INVESTIGATING SECOND GRADE

Thinking Kids®
Carson-Dellosa Publishing LLC
Greensboro, North Carolina

Thinking Kids®
Carson-Dellosa Publishing LLC
P.O. Box 35665
Greensboro, NC 27425 USA

ISBN 978-1-4838-3497-9

CONTENTS

ABOUT THIS BOOK

In **Investigating Second Grade**, your child will find hundreds of fun practice activities for essential math and language arts topics such as writing contractions and possessives, understanding place value, using irregular verbs, and counting money. All practice activities support current state educational standards for your child's grade level. Spending just a few minutes each day with this book will help your son or daughter grow in confidence and master important skills that lead to success at school.

But **Investigating Second Grade** is no ordinary workbook! It motivates students to learn with an intriguing mystery story to investigate and solve. While completing practice activities, your child will become a detective, collecting clues about suspects and answering vital questions about when, where, and how the mystery occurred. At the end of the book, your young investigator will put the clues together to crack the case!

Help your child follow these steps to become a second grade investigator:

1. **Read the Mystery Story: "The Mix-Up Mystery"**
   Read the mystery story beginning on page 6. Learn about where the mystery took place, what happened, and which suspects were witnessed at the scene. Look closely—you may find clues right in the story. Record clues in the **Detective's Notebook** on pages 202 and 203.

2. **Complete Learning Activities and Find Evidence**
   Complete skill-building math and language arts activities in each of four sections. On selected activity pages marked **Evidence Alert!**, solve puzzles to find evidence about the case. Keep track of the evidence you find. You will use it at the end of each section to discover a clue.

3. **Collect Clues**
   On the final page of each section, complete the **Clue Corner** activity. On this page, use all the evidence you found in the section to reveal a clue that answers a question such as

What? When? Where? How? or Who? Record each clue you find in the **Detective's Notebook** on pages 202 and 203.

4. **Record Clues in the Detective's Notebook**
   Each time you find a clue, record it in the **Detective's Notebook** on pages 202 and 203. Be sure to write clues exactly, one letter in each box shown. You will find clues to answer questions like these about the mystery: What happened? When did it happen? Where did it happen? How did it happen? and Who did it?

5. **Solve the Mystery**
   Use all the clues you collected to help complete the mystery story beginning on page 204. The letters you wrote inside green boxes in your **Detective's Notebook** will help you make choices. The choices you make will complete the story and solve the mystery. Congratulations, second grade investigator! You cracked the case and found clues about how to succeed at school, too!

Read the beginning of the mystery story. Then, follow the directions on page 8.

The Mix-Up Mystery

On a sunny Tuesday, Blenda Lott skipped happily along the sidewalk. School was out for the day. She was headed to her grandfather's new shop, Smoothie Station. She had been visiting the store for the past few weeks. On some days, she helped her grandfather and the other workers serve customers. On other days, he mixed up Blenda's favorite treat, a chocolate-banana-coconut smoothie.

As Blenda approached the store, she saw a customer burst out the front door and storm away. He had an angry look on his face. Blenda's grandfather followed the man. "Sorry!" he called out. "Please come again!"

Blenda stopped skipping. "What's wrong, Grandpa?" she asked.

"Everything!" he exclaimed. "A dozen customers have gone away angry today. They all said the same thing. They wanted to reorder the 'totally different, completely amazing, super tasty' smoothie they got here yesterday. But I have no idea what they are talking about! We do not have any new smoothies on the menu. I was at home all day yesterday. Someone else must have mixed up a new kind of smoothie and served it to customers.

But who? And why? And what was mixed in those delicious smoothies? I need answers!"

"Interesting," said Blenda. "What did these smoothies look like?"

"Some customers said they were orangey-blue. Others said they were reddish-green. A few people said the color was so unusual that it did not have a name."

"That is not much help," sighed Blenda. "What did the smoothies taste like?"

"Customers said they were sweet, but not too sweet. They were both creamy and icy. They were fruity, but no one could explain what kinds of **fruit** they contained. Without a recipe, there is no hope of making these stupendous smoothies again. Did they have papaya? Kumquat? Ugli fruit? I just don't know! Blenda, you are an extra-curious and extra-clever girl. Will you help solve this mystery? I have to leave the shop for a while. Could you find some clues about what was in those drinks?"

"Sure, Grandpa," promised Blenda. "I will have a look around and ask some questions. Who was here on **Monday**?"

"Mr. Solid and Trudy were here. Oh, and Ms. Wright, too," Blenda's grandfather said quickly. "I have to run now. Good luck!"

Blenda Lott thought about the people her grandfather named. Brock Solid was a friendly man who knew a lot about exercise and fitness. He helped Blenda's grandfather make sure that everything on the menu at Smoothie Station was packed with healthy ingredients.

Trudy Culors was a teenage girl who loved drawing and painting. Trudy was always thinking about her next art project. She worked at Smoothie Station when she was not at school.

Rita Ann Wright was a reporter for the local newspaper. Blenda knew that Ms. Wright was writing an article about the new smoothie shop in town.

Did one of these people know what was in the mysterious smoothies? It was time to find out.

BROCK SOLID

TRUDY CULORS

RITA ANN WRIGHT

It looks like this is a case for a second grade detective! Who mixed up the mysterious smoothies? What ingredients made them so delicious? It is up to you to collect clues and solve the mystery.

Look again at the story. Can you find clues in **bold** that answer these questions: **When** were the mystery smoothies sold? and **What** was in the smoothies? Write the clues in the **Detective's Notebook** on pages 202 and 203.

Now, keep going! Turn the page to complete learning activities, find evidence, collect clues, and solve the mystery.

TOP SECRET FILE #1:
Phonics and Spelling

Learning Goals:

- Review consonant sounds
- Distinguish between long and short vowel sounds in words
- Spell words with long vowel sounds
- Use apostrophes to write contractions and possessives
- Write compound words and other two-syllable words
- Use common spelling patterns to write words
- Write words with irregular spellings
- Use a dictionary

Collect Evidence on These Evidence Alert! Pages:
Pages 21, 31, 42, 53

Use Evidence to Find a Clue on the Clue Corner Page:
Page 58

Clue Question:
Where were the smoothies made?

A Consonant Begins It

Write a beginning consonant letter for each word. Color the pictures.

___orse

___ellyfish

___oat

___at

___ebra

___adybug

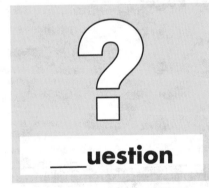

___uestion

___o-yo

___urtle

___est

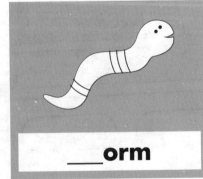

___orm

___cissors

Consonant Blends and Teams

Choose a consonant blend or team from the magnifying glass to complete each word.

_____ail

ch   ng
sn   tr
st   sh
wh   pl

_____ar

pea_____

_____um

ri_____

_____a_____

_____ale

_____ell

Short Vowel Review

Write **a**, **e**, **i**, **o**, or **u** to complete each word that has a short vowel sound.

___ctopus

s___n

k___ds

c___t

___lephant

d___g

sk___nk

___mbrella

p___n

Short Vowel Review

Write **a**, **e**, **i**, **o**, or **u** to complete each word that has a short vowel sound.

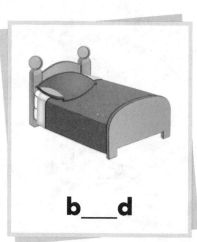

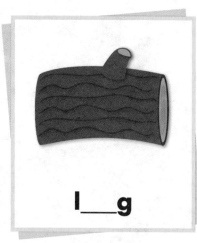

g___ft

b___t

m___n

p___mpkin

l___g

b___d

f___sh

b___b

___gg

Five Long Vowel Sounds

Write **a**, **e**, **i**, **o**, or **u** to help spell the words with long vowel sounds. Draw a line from each word to the matching picture. Color the pictures.

s___al

c___at

c___ke

c___be

k___te

Five Long Vowel Sounds

Write **a**, **e**, **i**, **o**, or **u** to help spell the words with long vowel sounds. Draw a line from each word to the matching picture. Color the pictures.

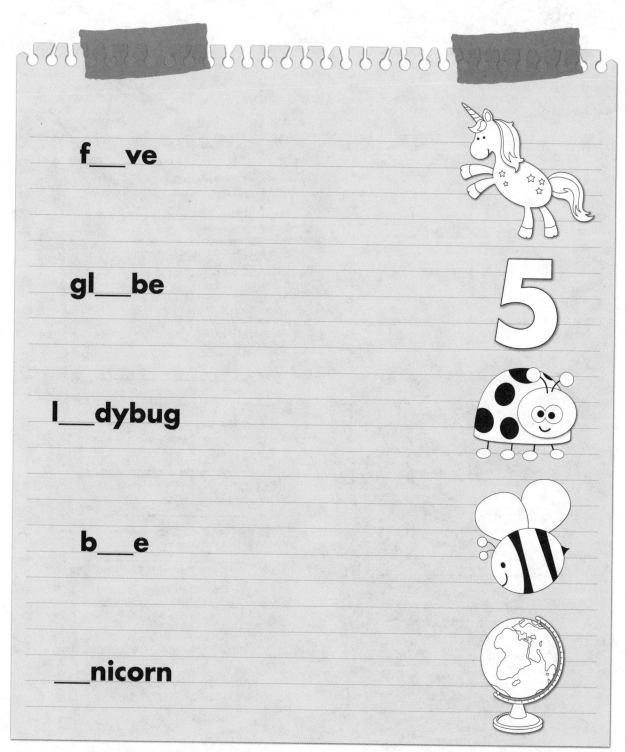

f__ve

gl__be

l__dybug

b__e

__nicorn

Long or Short?

Write the words with short vowel sounds on the short glass. Write the words with long vowel sounds on the tall glass.

mix	cup	lime	pay	seat
grape	price	shop	napkin	go

Long or Short?

Write the words with short vowel sounds on the short glass. Write the words with long vowel sounds on the tall glass.

| tomato | drink | sip | sweet | help |
| blend | kiwi | dates | ice | oats |

Letters and Sounds

Read each word. Follow the directions.

Circle the letters that spell the **long e** sound. **smoothie**	Circle the letter that spells the **short u** sound. **peanut**	Circle the letter that spells the **long a** sound. **station**
Circle the letters that spell the **long i** sound. **slice**	Circle the letter that spells the **short e** sound. **investigate**	Circle the letter that spells the **short i** sound. **milk**
Circle the letter that spells the **long e** sound. **berry**	Circle the letter that spells the **short a** sound. **back**	Circle the letter that spells the **long u** sound. **menu**

Mixed-Up Vowel Sounds

It is time to collect evidence about "The Mix-Up Mystery."

Blenda Lott looked around with a detective's eye. The front of the shop was clean and tidy. Neat stacks of fruits and vegetables stood behind the counter. Blenda noticed that one of the blenders was unplugged. That was strange. As Blenda fixed it, a customer came in. But, instead of coming up to place an order, he kept walking past the counter and stood in front of this.

Where did the customer stand? To find out, color the blenders that have words with long vowel sounds.

Look at the single letters on the blenders you colored. Write them, in order, to make a word that completes the sentence.

The customer stood near the _____ _____ _____ _____ in the corner of the shop.

You found evidence! Use the word you wrote to help you find a clue on page 58.

Long a Maze

Find a path from the fruit to the blender. Color each space that has a word with the **long a** sound.

neighbor	yard	writing	clean
Monday	cupcake	brother	ocean
buy	alien	table	flavor
party	asked	zebra	paid

Long a Spellings

What letters spell the **long a** sound in these words? Write each word under the matching spelling pattern.

eighteen	plain	amaze	shaky	away
paper	sunray	waited	brave	weighing

long a spelled a

_____

_____

long a spelled a-consonant-e

_____

_____

long a spelled ay

_____

_____

long a spelled ai

_____

_____

long a spelled ei

_____

_____

Search for Long e

Circle each word that has the **long e** sound. Then, find the words you circled in the puzzle.

even
leader
when
agree
waiter
delete
sleeping
pencil
fairly
writer
eagle
cherry

```
E Q Y B F G H C M J
A F S S R C D E V R
G A Z L N F E V E N
R I K E J C L S R Y
E R N E C H E R R Y
E L F P Y K T V N R
C Y B I D C E U M T
D L L N E A G L E Q
X E X G L E A D E R
L T G B C L F M Y V
```

Name

Long e Spellings

What letters spell the **long e** sound in these words? Write each word under the matching spelling pattern.

pretend peace	sorry greeting	complete kneel	equal these	please baby

long e spelled e

_____

_____

long e spelled e-consonant-e

_____

_____

long e spelled ee

_____

_____

long e spelled ea

_____

_____

long e spelled y

_____

_____

Long i Maze

Find a path from the fruit to the blender. Color each space that has a word with the **long i** sound.

flying	tonight	smiled	lake
create	igloo	July	hidden
slurped	creamy	sizes	three
finger	fake	white	pilot

Long i Spellings

What letters spell the **long i** sound in these words? Write each word under the matching spelling pattern.

supply tried	sideline delight	lie iron	nicely idea	tighten spy

long i spelled i

_____

_____

long i spelled i-consonant-e

_____

_____

long i spelled igh

_____

_____

long i spelled ie

_____

_____

long i spelled y

_____

_____

Search for Long o

Circle each word that has the **long o** sound. Then, find the words you circled in the puzzle.

potato
frown
snowy
robot
playing
hoped
goalie
lost
detective
window
frozen
toe

```
K A F O P O T A T O
L H R P M U M A D J
R H O P E D Q B E G
J I Z Y V L A V G O
H T E H V G V L R A
T J N W I N D O W L
V G X D J U H M I I
H U Y F W R G V E E
D T O E S N O W Y T
R O B O T M M Q O B
```

Long o Spellings

What letters spell the **long o** sound in these words? Write each word under the matching spelling pattern.

soapy broke	doe below	piano bonus	arrow alone	woe road

long o spelled o

_____

_____

long o spelled o-consonant-e

_____

_____

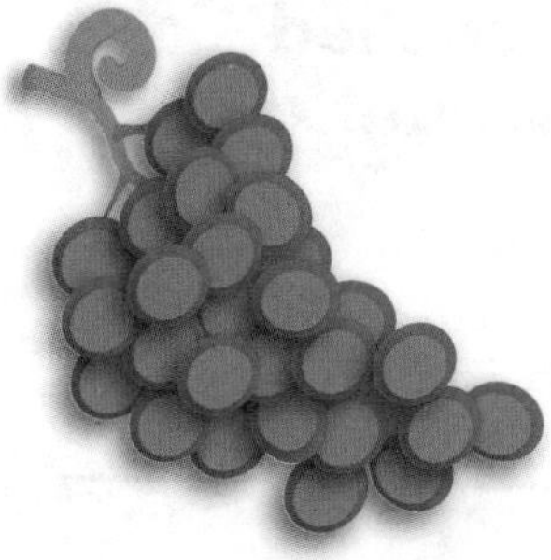

long o spelled ow

_____

_____

long o spelled oa

_____

_____

long o spelled oe

_____

_____

Long u Words

Find a path from the fruit to the blender. Color each space that has a word with the **long u** sound. Then, write each word you colored under the matching spelling pattern.

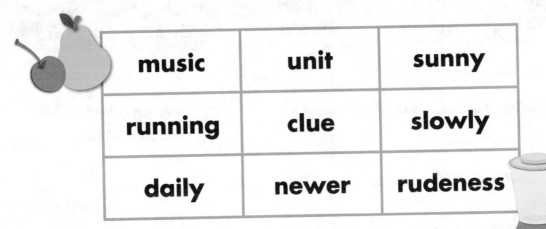

music	unit	sunny
running	clue	slowly
daily	newer	rudeness

long u spelled u

_____

_____

long u spelled u-consonant-e

_____

long u spelled ue

_____

long u spelled ew

_____

Look for Long Vowels

Evidence ALERT!

It is time to collect more evidence about "The Mix-Up Mystery."

Blenda Lott politely directed the customer to the front counter. The man wasn't happy that he could not order the same outstanding smoothie he got yesterday, but he chose something from the menu and left satisfied. Why did he first go to the door in the corner, Blenda wondered. The door leading to the back of the shop was for workers only. It had a pass-through window that was always latched shut. Blenda looked closely at the latch. What did she notice? To find out, write vowel letters to complete the long vowel words. Use the symbols to write a letter in each magnifying glass.

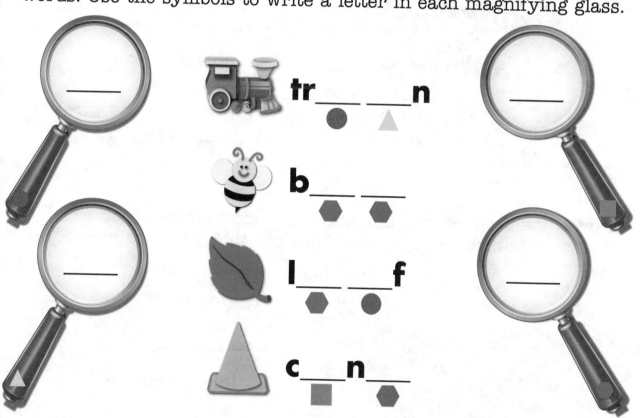

tr___ ___n

b___ ___

l___ ___f

c___n___

Use the code to complete the word and finish the sentence.

Blenda noticed that the latch was ___p___n.

You found evidence! Use the word you wrote to help you find a clue on page 58.

I Spy Syllables

Look at the words on the note. Draw a line between the double consonants to divide each word into two syllables. Do you notice that each syllable contains a vowel sound? Write each word under its two vowel sounds.

yellow

puppy

mitten

coffee

short i | short e

_____

short e | long o

_____

short u | long e

_____

short o | long e

_____

Draw a line between two unlike consonants to divide each word into two syllables. Then, write each word under its two vowel sounds.

snowcone

candy

subtract

rainbow

long a | long o

_____

long o | long o

_____

short a | long e

_____

short u | short a

_____

R in Control

The letter **r** can change the vowel sound in a word. The vowel sound in **her** is an **r**-controlled vowel. Write an **r**-controlled word to complete each sentence.

1. The color of a berry-blast smoothie is _____.

2. Customers can _____ their cars in the lot behind Smoothie Station.

3. There are four _____ for each table in the shop.

park   purple

girl   shirts

store   chairs

4. Blenda Lott is an extra-curious and extra-clever _____.

5. All the workers at Smoothie Station wear yellow _____.

6. A new _____ opened in our town.

Vowel Teams

Vowel pairs, or teams, can make different sounds in different words. Write a vowel team to complete each word.

p____l

b____n

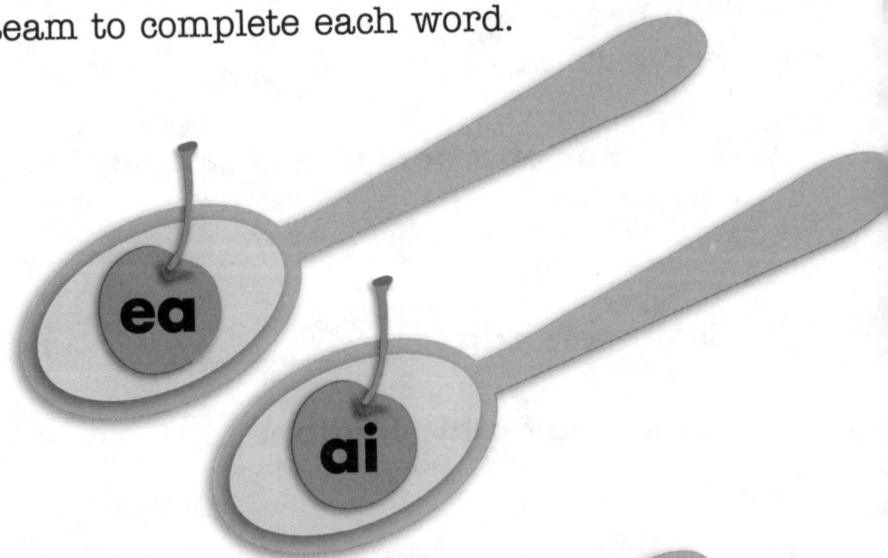

ea

ai

cl____d

c____se

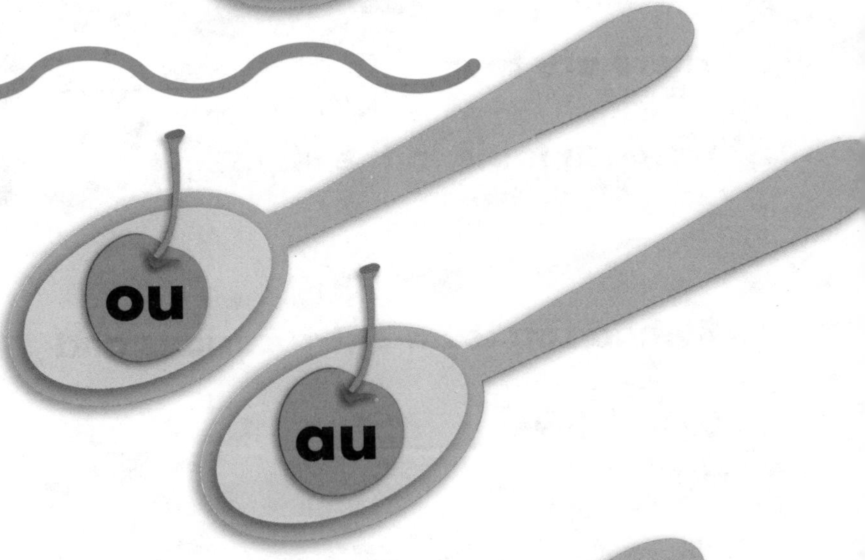

ou

au

s____son

w____ther

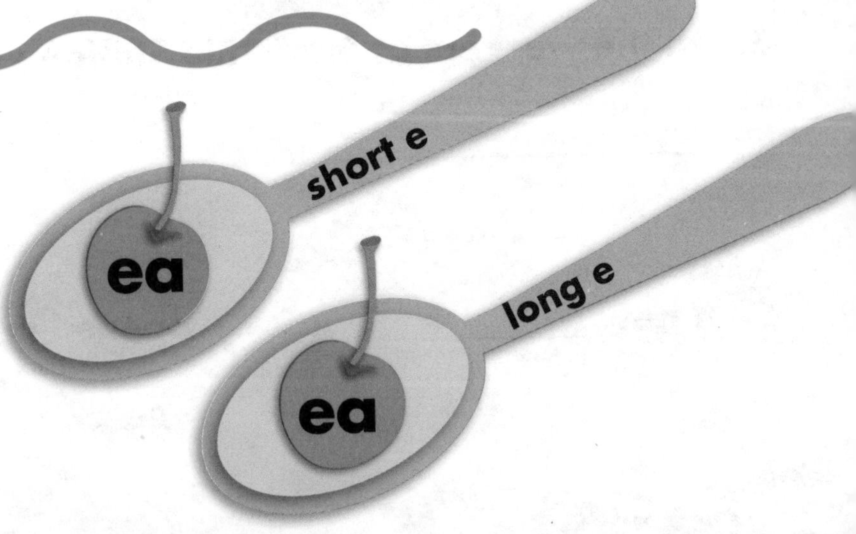

ea short e

ea long e

Vowel Teams

Write a vowel team to complete each word.

____ther

bel____ve

f____l

b____

f____t

c____t

Y Can Be a Vowel

When **y** comes at the end of a word, it is a vowel. If it is a one-syllable word, **y** makes a **long i** sound (as in **my**). If it is a two-syllable word, **y** makes a **long e** sound (as in **baby**). Write each word under its vowel sound.

| happy | fry | sleepy | bunny | windy | party |
| penny | try | dry | why | sky | fly |

long i

long e

Silent Letters

Some words have consonant letters you can't hear at all, such as **gh** in **right**, **w** in **wrong**, **l** in **walk**, **k** in **knife**, **b** in **climb**, or **t** in **listen**. Write a word for each picture. Underline the silent letters. If a word does not have a picture, draw one.

night ballet	calf comb	wrench thumb	lamb eight	knee

_____

_____

_____

_____

_____

_____

_____

_____

_____

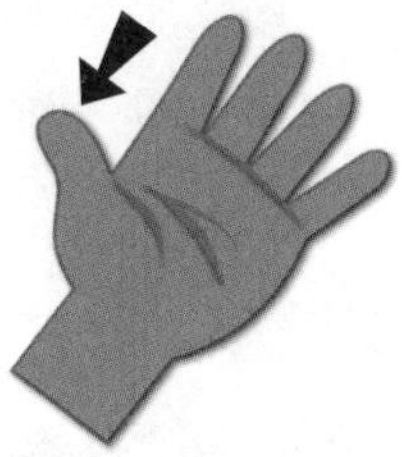

Hard and Soft c

When **c** is followed by **e**, **i**, or **y** in a word, it often has a soft sound that sounds like the letter **s** (examples: **circle**, **fence**). When **c** is followed by **a**, **o**, or **u** in a word, it often has a hard sound that sounds like the letter **k** (examples: **cup**, **cart**). Write each word under the sound that **c** makes.

| captain | popcorn | candy | cardboard | cent | ceiling |
| decide | princess | cupcake | suitcase | celery | spicy |

Soft c Sound

Hard c Sound

_____   _____

_____   _____

_____   _____

_____   _____

_____   _____

Hard and Soft g

When **g** is followed by **e**, **i**, or **y** in a word, it often has a soft sound that sounds like the letter **j** (examples: **change**, **gem**). When **g** is followed by **a**, **o**, or **u** in a word, it often has a hard sound (examples: **go**, **gum**). Write each word under the sound that **g** makes.

| gentle | guest | giant | damage | digit | giving |
| guitar | gate | engine | goldfish | magic | goose |

Soft g Sound

Hard g Sound

_____

_____

_____

_____

_____

_____

Compound Words

Some words can be put together to make compound words. Read each small word. Put the words together to make compound words.

sun + flower = _____

horse + shoe = _____

dog + house = _____

tooth + brush = _____

rain + bow = _____

Compound Words

Read each small word. Put the words together to make compound words.

 +  =

pan + **cake** = _____

 +  =

snow + **man** = _____

 +  =

wheel + **chair** = _____

 + =

fish + **bowl** = _____

 + =

mail + **box** = _____

Compound Code

It is time to collect more evidence about "The Mix-Up Mystery."

Blenda went through the door and began to investigate the back of the shop. In a corner stood her grandfather's messy desk. Tall shelves held boxes of ingredients. A long work table in the center of the room was usually clean, but today it was not. On the tabletop, Blenda found a lemon peel, a pen with purple ink, and a stack of these. What was stacked on the table? To find out, write letters in the circles to make compound words that answer the questions.

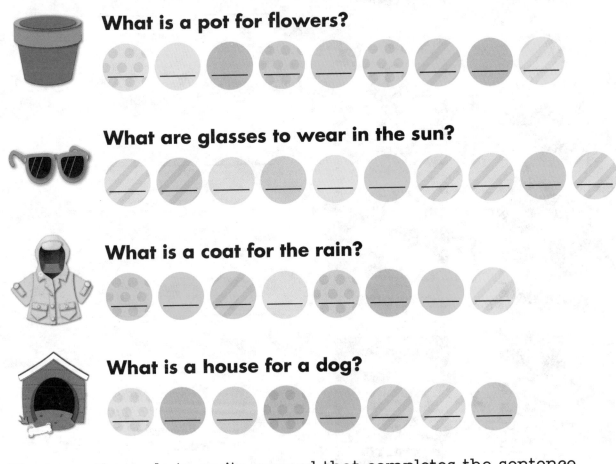

What is a pot for flowers?

◯ ◯ ◯ ◯ ◯ ◯ ◯ ◯ ◯

What are glasses to wear in the sun?

◯ ◯ ◯ ◯ ◯ ◯ ◯ ◯ ◯

What is a coat for the rain?

◯ ◯ ◯ ◯ ◯ ◯ ◯ ◯

What is a house for a dog?

◯ ◯ ◯ ◯ ◯ ◯ ◯ ◯

Now, use the code to write a word that completes the sentence.

Blenda found ◯◯◯◯ stacked on the table.

You found evidence! Use the word you wrote to help you find a clue on page 58.

Step Up to Compound Words

Combine words from the footprints to make compound words.
Write the new words on the lines.

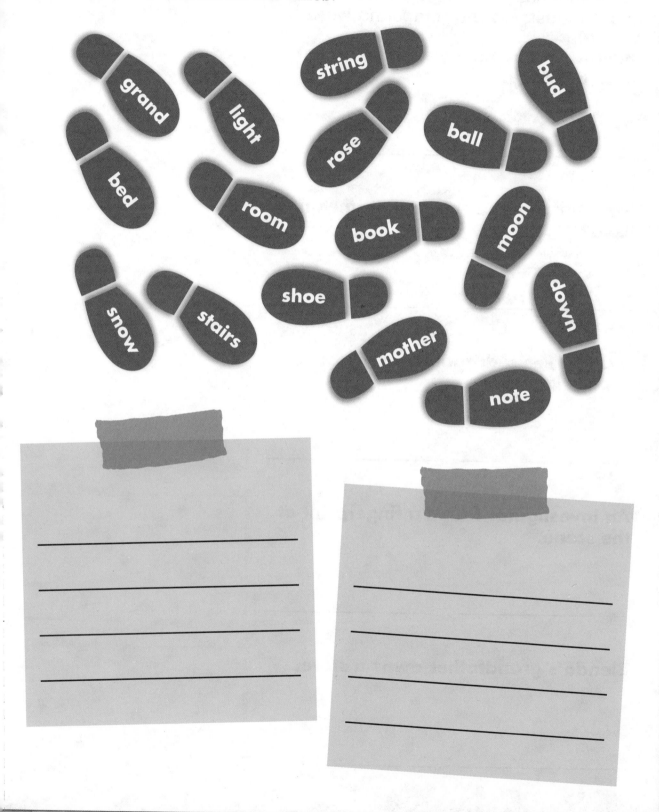

Picture It!

First, underline the compound word in each sentence. Next, write the two smaller words that make it up. Last, draw a picture in the box to illustrate the compound word.

Blenda will be nine years old on her next birthday.

_____ _____

How far can you spit a watermelon seed?

_____ _____

Did you see a dragonfly at the pond?

_____ _____

An investigator found a fingerprint at the scene.

_____ _____

Blenda's grandfather owns a store.

_____ _____

Contraction Swap

Circle two words in each sentence that could be replaced by the contraction.

She is searching for clues.

It is time to go home.

Blenda will not give up.

I can not wait to play the game.

The customer was not happy.

The question has not been answered.

Contraction Subtraction

Use the words on the handle of each magnifying glass to make a contraction that completes the sentence. Subtract the letters in **blue** and replace them with an apostrophe (').

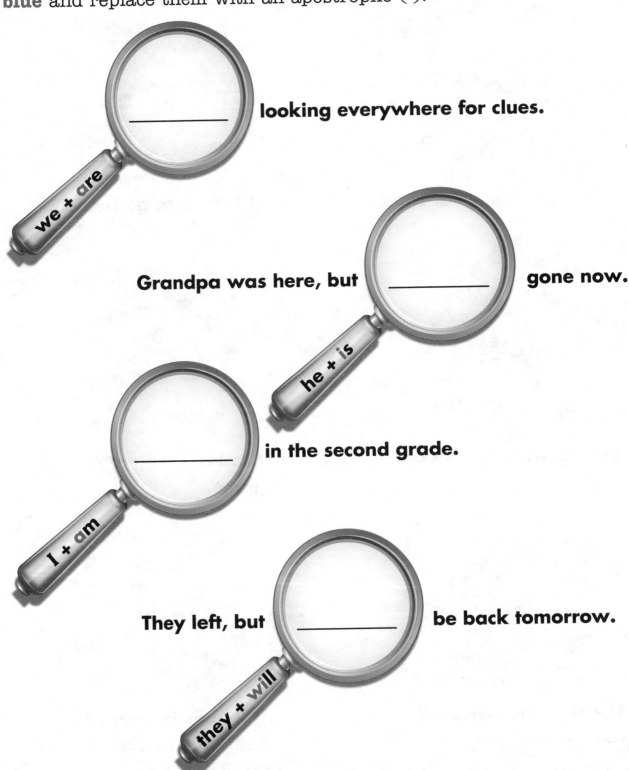

_____ looking everywhere for clues.

we + are

Grandpa was here, but _____ gone now.

he + is

_____ in the second grade.

I + am

They left, but _____ be back tomorrow.

they + will

Contraction Subtraction

Use the words on the handle of each magnifying glass to make a contraction that completes the sentence. Subtract the letters in **blue** and replace them with an apostrophe (').

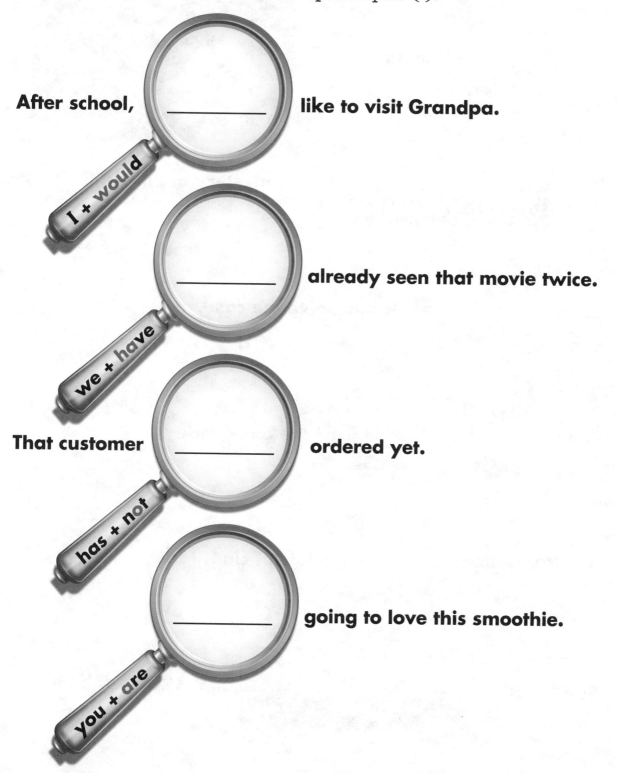

After school, _____ like to visit Grandpa.

I + would

_____ already seen that movie twice.

we + have

That customer _____ ordered yet.

has + not

_____ going to love this smoothie.

you + are

Complete the Contractions

Write letters in each set of boxes to make contractions that complete the sentences.

1. Hi, ☐'☐ Blenda Lott.
   I am

2. ☐☐☐☐☐'☐ a mystery at Smoothie Station.
   There   is

3. ☐☐'☐ my job to solve the case.
   It is

4. I ☐☐☐☐'☐ here on Monday.
   was   not

5. I know ☐'☐☐ find lots of clues today.
   I will

6. I am glad ☐☐☐'☐☐ on the case with me!
   you   are

Who Owns It?

Possessive nouns show ownership. An apostrophe and **s** (**'s**) at the end of the noun show who or what owns something. Draw a line to match each possessive noun with the thing that is owned.

the detective's

Grandfather's

a customer's

Blenda's

the table's

that blender's

change

questions

plug

notebook

chair

Smoothie Station

store

Possessive Practice

Rewrite each sentence, changing the words in color to include a possessive noun that ends in apostrophe **s** (**'s**).

The party of Trey was at Smoothie Station.

_____

The **theme of the party** was space explorers.

_____

The **decorations of the cake** were awesome.

_____

The **treats of the day** were galaxy grape smoothies.

_____

Eight of the **friends of the birthday boy** came.

_____

Possessive Practice

Rewrite each sentence, changing the words in color to include a possessive noun that ends in apostrophe **s** (**'s**).

The rules of a silly game made everyone laugh.

_____

The favor for each friend was an alien action figure.

_____

The gift of Regina to Trey was a board game.

_____

The gift of Samuel to Trey was a sticker book.

_____

The gift of Raj to Trey was a solar system T-shirt.

_____

Where Does the Apostrophe Go?

Circle the correct phrase to describe ownership.

the store's sign
the stores sign's

the astronauts suits'
the astronaut's suit

the planets ring's
the planet's rings

the cakes frostings
the cake's frosting

the alien's ship
the aliens ship's

the gifts bow's
the gift's bow

Name

Apostrophes A to Z

Evidence ALERT!

It is time to collect more evidence about "The Mix-Up Mystery."

   That was strange, Blenda thought. Cups belonged in the front of the store where the smoothies were made, not in the back. Blenda looked closer at the work table. Some white seeds were stuck to the tabletop near the cups. Under the table, Blenda found a scrap of paper covered in purple marks. She noticed that the floor under her feet did not feel right. How did it feel? To find out, circle a letter in each word. If it is a possessive noun, circle the letter closest to **a** in the alphabet. If it is a contraction, circle the letter closest to **z** in the alphabet.

she'll
it's
Lin's
school's
Kylo's
you're

Now, write each letter you circled, in order, to make a word that completes the sentence.

The floor under the table felt ____ ____ ____ ____ ____ ____.

You found evidence! Use the word you wrote to help you find a clue on page 58.

In the Bag

Write the words on the bags in ABC order.

grapes   _____

bread   _____

soup   _____

apples   _____

napkins   _____

rolls   _____

ice cream   _____

pizza   _____

carrots   _____

bananas   _____

treats   _____

potatoes   _____

rice   _____

soda   _____

cups   _____

beans   _____

Name

In Order

Write the words on the lines in ABC order. If two words start with the same letter, look at the second letter in each word.

tree   _____

branch   _____

leaf   _____

rain   _____

umbrella   _____

cloud   _____

dish   _____

dog   _____

bone   _____

mail   _____

stamp   _____

slot   _____

Look It Up!

Use the dictionary page to answer the questions.

smelly (*adj.*) Having a bad odor. smell•y

smile (*noun*) A happy or pleased expression in which a person's lips are curved up. (*verb*) To form a smile by curving the lips up. smile

smock (*noun*) A long, loose piece of fabric worn over clothes to protect them. smock

smog (*noun*) A mixture of fog and smoke. smog

smoky (*adj.*) Full of smoke or giving off smoke. smok•y

smolder (*verb*) To burn slowly without flames. smol•der

smooth (*adj.*) 1. Not rough or uneven. 2. Moving without sudden stops and starts. (*verb*) To make smooth. smooth

smoothie (*noun*) A drink made by blending fruit, ice, and other ingredients. smooth•ie

What is worn to protect clothes?_____

What word could you use to describe a car ride with no sudden

stops or starts?_____

What word names an expression you might see on someone's

face? _____

How many syllables does smoothie have? _____

What word spells the long i sound i-consonant-e?_____

Name

Look It Up!

Use the dictionary page to answer the questions.

muss (*verb*) To make messy or untidy. muss

mustache (*noun*) Hair growing on the upper lip. mus•tache

mustard (*noun*) A spicy sauce made from the seeds of the mustard plant. mus•tard

musty (*adj.*) Having a damp and rotten smell. must•y

mute (*adj.*) Silent or unspoken. (*noun*) A device used to soften the sound of a musical instrument. (*verb*) To muffle or soften sound. mute

mutt (*noun*) A mixed-breed dog. mutt

mystery (*noun*) 1. Something that is not understood or is kept a secret. 2. A story about uncovering a secret. mys•ter•y

myth (*noun*) A very old story. myth

What is a sauce to put on food? _____

What word could you use to describe a dark, wet place? _____
_____

What word might a musician use? _____

How many syllables does mystery **have?** _____

What two-syllable word ends with the long e **sound?** _____
_____

CLUE CORNER

Meaning Match

It is time to find a clue about "The Mix-Up Mystery"!

Blenda Lott thought about the evidence she had so far. She remembered the customer at the unlatched window. She thought about the unplugged blender, the items on the table that were out of place, and the messy floor. Adding it all up, she came to a logical conclusion about where the mysterious smoothies were made. What did Blenda decide? To find out, write the words you gathered as evidence on pages 21, 31, 42, and 53 in the **green** spaces. Then, choose one word to write in all the **purple** spaces.

> **awkward**: 1. Clumsy. 2. Hard to handle.
>
> **back**: 1. Away from the front. 2. Return to how it was.
>
> **bad**: 1. Not good. 2. Incorrect.
>
> **basic**: 1. Important. 2. The main part.

The _____ of a stamp is _____.

The swimming pool closed in August, but now it is

_____ _____.

There was wet paint on the front porch, so I went to the

_____ _____.

Please put these _____ in the _____ of the cupboard.

What word did you write in the **purple** spaces? Write it again to finish the sentence and find a clue.

Clue: Where were the smoothies made?
The mysterious smoothies must have been made in the _____ of the store.

Write the clue word you found in the Detective's Notebook on pages 202 and 203.

Name

TOP SECRET FILE #2:
Addition, Subtraction, and Place Value

Learning Goals:

- Add and subtract within 1,000
- Find the total number of objects in rows and columns
- Understand odd and even
- Solve word problems
- Understand place value to hundreds
- Skip-count by fives, tens, and hundreds
- Read and write numbers in different ways
- Compare three-digit numbers

Collect Evidence on These Evidence Alert! Pages:
Pages 68, 76, 88, 98

Use Evidence to Find a Clue on the Clue Corner Page:
Page 106

Clue Question:
Who did it?

Suspect:
Rita Ann Wright

You Got This!

Add from memory.

$$3 + 4$$

$$8 + 2$$

$$5 + 7$$

$$2 + 1$$

$$9 + 7$$

$$9 + 9$$

$$6 + 2$$

$$4 + 8$$

$$8 + 7$$

$$5 + 5$$

$$6 + 8$$

$$9 + 4$$

$$7 + 4$$

$$5 + 9$$

$$3 + 8$$

$$6 + 7$$

Two Equal Shares?

Can each set of writing supplies be divided into two equal groups?
Answer the questions.

What number is shown? _____
Is the number odd or even?
Circle one: **odd   even**

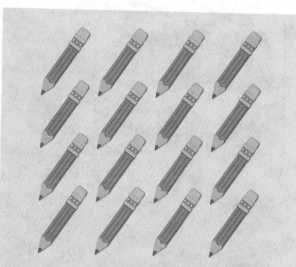

What number is shown? _____
Is the number odd or even?
Circle one: **odd   even**

What number is shown? _____
Is the number odd or even?
Circle one: **odd   even**

What number is shown? _____
Is the number odd or even?
Circle one: **odd   even**

One Left Over?

Circle pairs of objects in each set. Is one object left over? Complete the equation to show the number. Write the same addends (doubles) in the blanks. Then, answer the question. The first one is done for you.

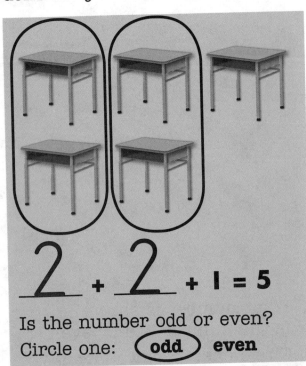

$$\underline{2} + \underline{2} + 1 = 5$$

Is the number odd or even?

Circle one: (odd)   even

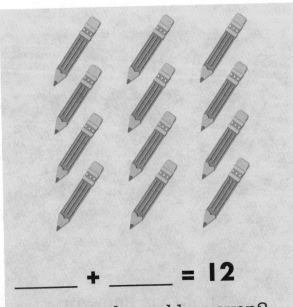

$$\underline{} + \underline{} = 12$$

Is the number odd or even?

Circle one: odd   even

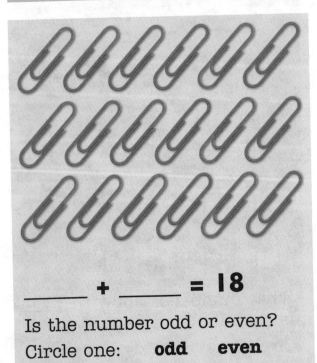

$$\underline{} + \underline{} = 18$$

Is the number odd or even?

Circle one: odd   even

$$\underline{} + \underline{} + 1 = 7$$

Is the number odd or even?

Circle one: odd   even

One Left Over?

Circle pairs of objects in each set. Is one object left over? Complete the equation to show the number. Write the same addends (doubles) in the blanks. Then, answer the question.

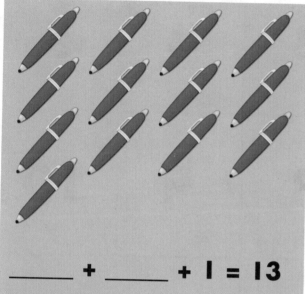

_____ + _____ + 1 = 13

Is the number odd or even?
Circle one:　**odd**　**even**

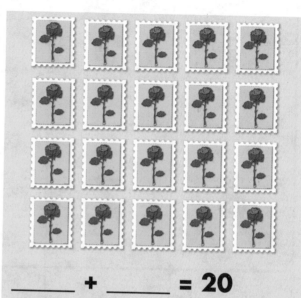

_____ + _____ = 20

Is the number odd or even?
Circle one:　**odd**　**even**

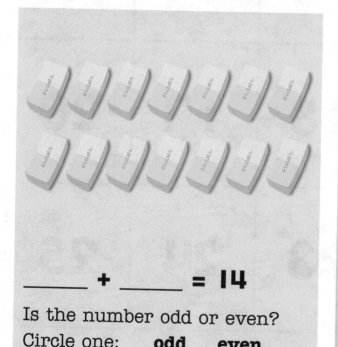

_____ + _____ = 14

Is the number odd or even?
Circle one:　**odd**　**even**

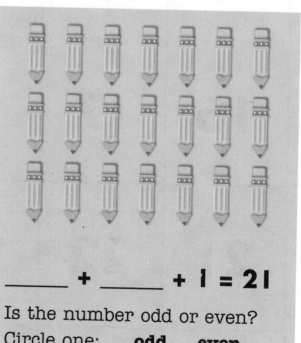

_____ + _____ + 1 = 21

Is the number odd or even?
Circle one:　**odd**　**even**

Color Chart

Color the even numbers **red**. Color the odd numbers **blue**.

1	2	3	4	5
6	7	8	9	10
11	12	13	14	15
16	17	18	19	20
21	22	23	24	25

Name

Solve and Draw

Draw a number of items in rows and columns to match each problem. Solve the problem. Then, answer the question.

4 + 4 + 4 + 4 = _____

Is the number odd or even?
Circle one: **odd   even**

7 + 7 + 7 = _____

Is the number odd or even?
Circle one: **odd   even**

5 + 5 + 5 + 5 = _____

Is the number odd or even?
Circle one: **odd   even**

9 + 9 + 9 = _____

Is the number odd or even?
Circle one: **odd   even**

An Even Count

It is time to collect more evidence about "The Mix-Up Mystery."

   I know where the mystery smoothies were made, thought Blenda, but who made them? Just then, the newspaper reporter Rita Ann Wright came bustling into the store's back room. "Hello, dear," she said to Blenda as she pulled a notebook and a blue pen from her bag. "I know your grandfather isn't here, but I need to work on my article. I'll just have a look around." Ms. Wright began to pick things up. "What is this?" she asked as she held up a whisk. "I've never seen one before." How many things did Ms. Wright pick up? To find out, circle the even numbers.

Name

Evidence ALERT!

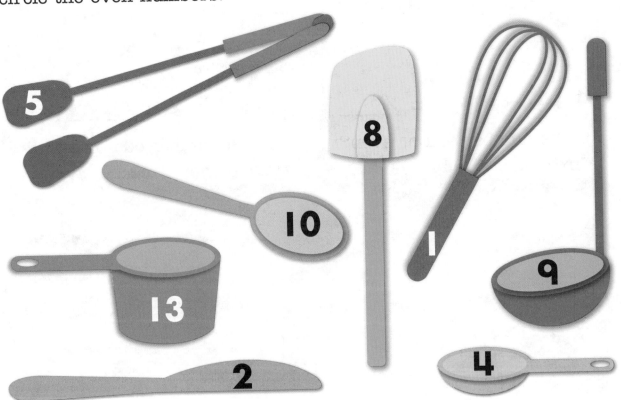

Write the sum of the numbers you circled to complete the sentence.

Rita Ann Wright picked up _____ things in the back room of Smoothie Station.

You found evidence! Use the number you wrote to help you find a clue on page 106.

Twenty Plus

Circle the two numbers in each problem that equal 20. Then, write the third number in the equation and find the sum. Add the tens. Then, add the ones. The first one is done for you.

$12 + \boxed{18} + \boxed{2} = 20 + 12 = 32$

$13 + 29 + 7 = 20 + \square = \square$

$8 + 80 + 12 = 20 + \square = \square$

$10 + 67 + 10 = 20 + \square = \square$

$14 + 6 + 41 = 20 + \square = \square$

$11 + 59 + 9 = 20 + \square = \square$

$4 + 78 + 16 = 20 + \square = \square$

Addition Breakdown

Add by breaking the second number into tens and ones. Then, add the ones and add the groups of tens. The first two have been started for you.

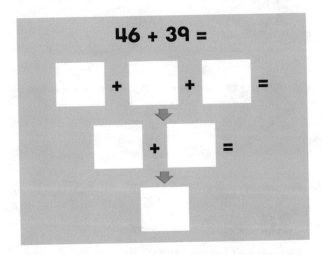

56 + 23 =

56 + 20 + 3 =

76 + 3 =

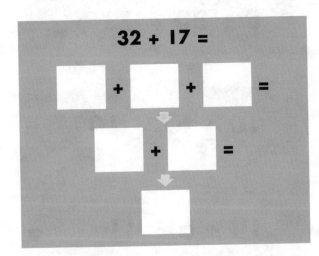

28 + 14 =

28 + 10 + 4 =

⬜ + ⬜ =

⬜

46 + 39 =

⬜ + ⬜ + ⬜ =

⬜ + ⬜ =

⬜

32 + 17 =

⬜ + ⬜ + ⬜ =

⬜ + ⬜ =

⬜

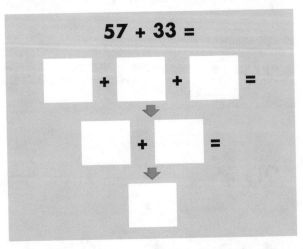

57 + 33 =

⬜ + ⬜ + ⬜ =

⬜ + ⬜ =

⬜

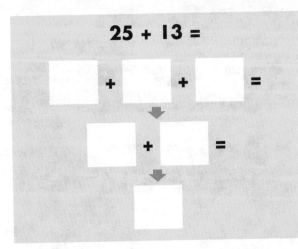

25 + 13 =

⬜ + ⬜ + ⬜ =

⬜ + ⬜ =

⬜

Subtraction Square

Use the hundred board to help you subtract. Put your finger on the first number. Count back the number of squares shown by the second number to find the difference.

31	57	19	77	99	88
− 10	− 13	− 8	− 12	− 6	− 10

22	67	36	88	94	51
− 11	− 14	− 9	− 12	− 5	− 12

1	2	3	4	5	6	7	8	9	10
11	12	13	14	15	16	17	18	19	20
21	22	23	24	25	26	27	28	29	30
31	32	33	34	35	36	37	38	39	40
41	42	43	44	45	46	47	48	49	50
51	52	53	54	55	56	57	58	59	60
61	62	63	64	65	66	67	68	69	70
71	72	73	74	75	76	77	78	79	80
81	82	83	84	85	86	87	88	89	90
91	92	93	94	95	96	97	98	99	100

Ones, Then Tens

To solve each problem, add or subtract the ones. Then, add or subtract the tens. Regroup tens as needed.

$$\begin{array}{r} 45 \\ + 37 \\ \hline \end{array}$$
$$\begin{array}{r} 23 \\ - 5 \\ \hline \end{array}$$
$$\begin{array}{r} 38 \\ + 46 \\ \hline \end{array}$$
$$\begin{array}{r} 57 \\ + 15 \\ \hline \end{array}$$

$$\begin{array}{r} 80 \\ - 42 \\ \hline \end{array}$$
$$\begin{array}{r} 85 \\ - 37 \\ \hline \end{array}$$
$$\begin{array}{r} 55 \\ + 6 \\ \hline \end{array}$$
$$\begin{array}{r} 63 \\ - 57 \\ \hline \end{array}$$

$$\begin{array}{r} 83 \\ - 9 \\ \hline \end{array}$$
$$\begin{array}{r} 64 \\ + 27 \\ \hline \end{array}$$
$$\begin{array}{r} 94 \\ - 67 \\ \hline \end{array}$$
$$\begin{array}{r} 64 \\ + 27 \\ \hline \end{array}$$

$$\begin{array}{r} 77 \\ - 19 \\ \hline \end{array}$$
$$\begin{array}{r} 44 \\ + 19 \\ \hline \end{array}$$
$$\begin{array}{r} 52 \\ - 24 \\ \hline \end{array}$$
$$\begin{array}{r} 12 \\ + 48 \\ \hline \end{array}$$

At Smoothie Station

Add or subtract to solve the word problems.

Blenda Lott is 9 years old. Rita Ann Wright is 27 years old. How much older is Ms. Wright?

☐ years

A truck brought 26 boxes of supplies on Monday and 37 boxes of supplies on Friday. How many boxes of supplies were delivered in all?

☐ boxes

A school class with 26 students visited Smoothie Station. The workers had prepared 32 treats for them. How many treats were left over?

☐ treats

Rita Ann Wright has 96 hours to finish her story about Smoothie Station. She has been working on the story for 68 hours. How many hours does she have left?

☐ hours

On a Saturday, 32 customers ordered a smoothie with strawberries. 58 customers ordered a smoothie without strawberries. How many customers ordered a smoothie on that day?

☐ customers

A gumball machine in the shop holds 75 gumballs. 48 gumballs are in the machine. How many gumballs have been sold since the machine was full?

☐ gumballs

Sum Smoothie!

It is time to collect more evidence about "The Mix-Up Mystery."

Rita Ann Wright kept snooping around and scribbling notes. As she bent to look under a shelf, a take-out menu fell from her bag. "Thanks," said Ms. Wright when Blenda picked it up. "I will need that. I never have time to cook!"

"Have you ever made a smoothie?" asked Blenda.

"Yes! Your grandfather showed me how on Sunday. It was fun tossing all kinds of fruits into the blender. It was my own unique creation. And the taste was fascinating!"

"How many different ingredients did you put in?" asked Blenda. To find the answer, write numbers in the squares so that the sum of each row, column, and diagonal is the same.

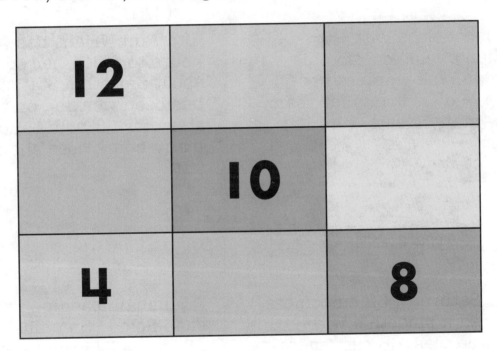

What is the sum of each row, column, and diagonal? Write the number to complete the sentence.

Rita Ann Wright put _____ different ingredients in her smoothie.

You found evidence! Use the number you wrote to help you find a clue on page 106.

Ten Tens Is 100

Ten tens equal 100. Look at each group of hundreds blocks. Write the number shown. The first one is done for you. Hint: Each number you write will end with 00.

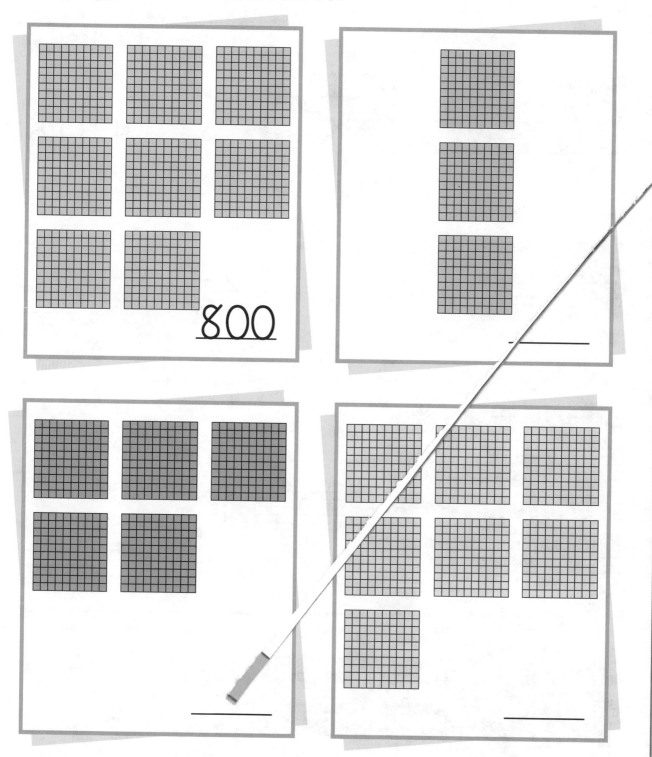

800

Three Places

Write the three-digit number shown by each set of blocks. The first one is done for you.

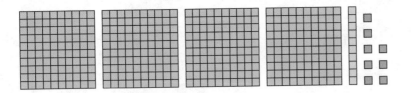 = 418

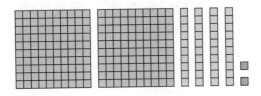 = ___

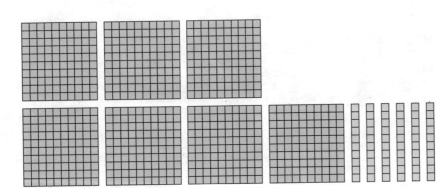 = ___

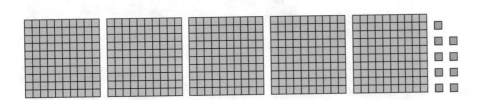 = ___

Three Places

Write the three-digit number shown by each set of blocks.

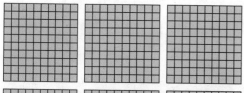
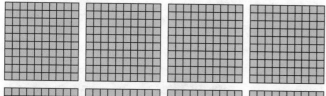

 = _____

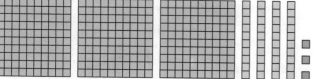
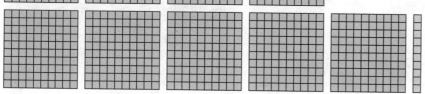

 = _____

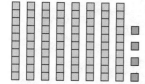

 = _____

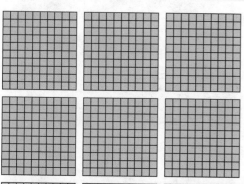
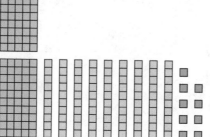

 = _____

Make It Big!

Write each set of three numbers in the boxes. Choose the order for the digits that will make the largest number possible.

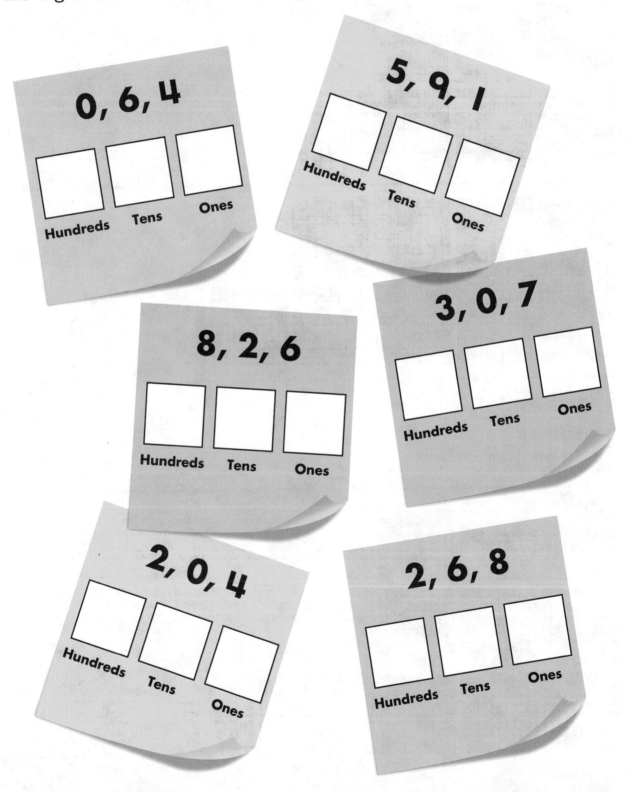

0, 6, 4

Hundreds Tens Ones

5, 9, 1

Hundreds Tens Ones

8, 2, 6

Hundreds Tens Ones

3, 0, 7

Hundreds Tens Ones

2, 0, 4

Hundreds Tens Ones

2, 6, 8

Hundreds Tens Ones

Name

Make It Small!

Write each set of three numbers in the boxes. Choose the order for the digits that will make the smallest number possible. Hint: If you decide to write 0 in the hundreds place or the tens place, you can leave that box blank.

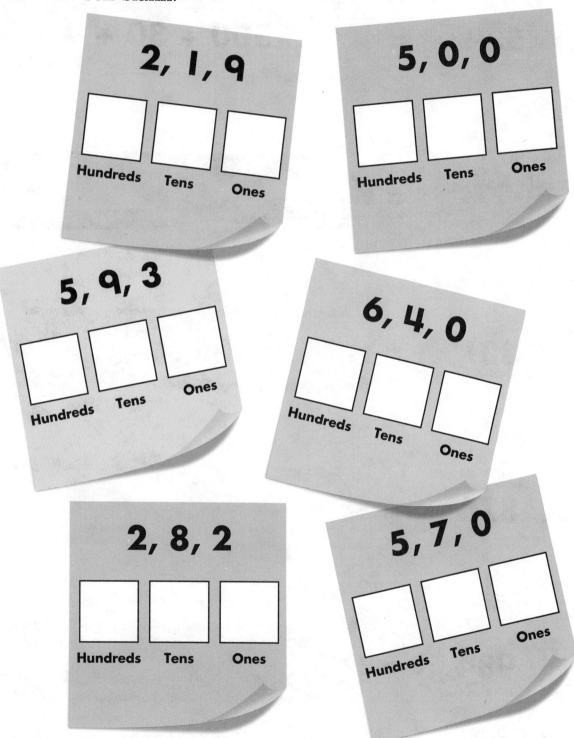

Expanding Numbers

Write each number in expanded form. The first one is done for you.

534 = 500 + 30 + 4

27 =

301 =

876 =

984 =

Expanding Numbers

Write each number in expanded form.

435 = [   ]

202 = [   ]

68 = [   ]

732 = [   ]

851 = [   ]

Take Note!

Help Rita Ann Wright take notes. For each number name, write a numeral on the notebook.

six hundred twenty-nine

four hundred eight

sixteen

nine hundred seventy

seven hundred sixty-one

two hundred eleven

Numbers Have Names

Write a number name for each numeral. The first one is done for you. Hint: Do not use the word **and**. When the digits in the tens and ones places form a number greater than 20, write a hyphen (–) between their names.

968

nine hundred sixty-eight

452

_____

74

_____

506

_____

380

_____

Matching Prints

Draw lines to match the numbers.

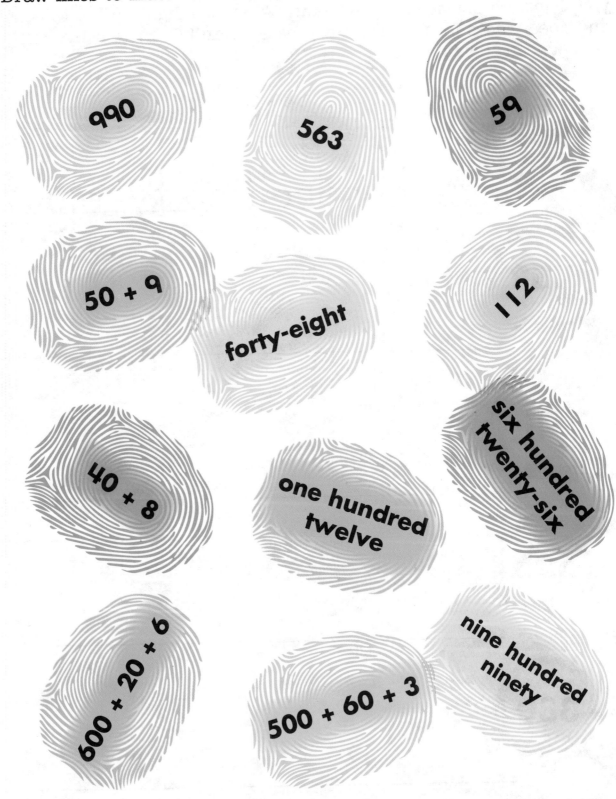

990

563

59

50 + 9

forty-eight

112

40 + 8

one hundred twelve

six hundred twenty-six

600 + 20 + 6

500 + 60 + 3

nine hundred ninety

Matching Prints

Draw lines to match the numbers.

128

75

616

300 + 8

500 + 60 + 7

567

six hundred sixteen

four hundred ninety-eight

three hundred eight

100 + 20 + 8

seventy-five

400 + 90 + 8

Reading Riddles

It is time to collect more evidence about "The Mix-Up Mystery."

"My smoothie creation was so interesting, I wanted to tell my readers about it," continued Rita Ann Wright. "That's why I posted a story about it Sunday night on my blog at the newspaper's website. I wrote all about how I made the smoothie. I even included a video! Lots of people read the blog post. They are looking forward to reading my big article about Smoothie Station."

"How many people read your blog post?" asked Blenda. To find the answer, solve the riddles.

Name

- When counting by twos, count twice to find my ones digit.
- My tens digit is twice my ones digit.
- My hundreds digit is 1 less than my ones digit

What number am I?

Hundreds	Tens	Ones

- When counting by threes, count twice to find my hundreds digit.
- My ones digit is half my hundreds digit.
- My tens digit is the sum of my hundreds and ones digits.

What number am I?

Hundreds	Tens	Ones

Look at the two numbers you wrote. Which one has a tens digit with a value of 80? Write it to complete the sentence.

Rita Ann Wright's blog post was read by _____ people.

You found evidence! Use the number you wrote to help you find a clue on page 106.

Greatest, Least, or Equal?

Circle the largest number.

567

five hundred seventy-six

500 + 50 + 6

Circle the smallest number.

three hundred twenty-nine

399

300 + 20 + 3

Circle the numbers that are equal.

700 + 80 + 2

seven hundred twenty-eight

728

Can You Compare?

Compare the numbers. First, look at the hundreds digits. Then, look at the tens digits. Finally, look at the ones digits. Write >, <, or = in each magnifying glass.

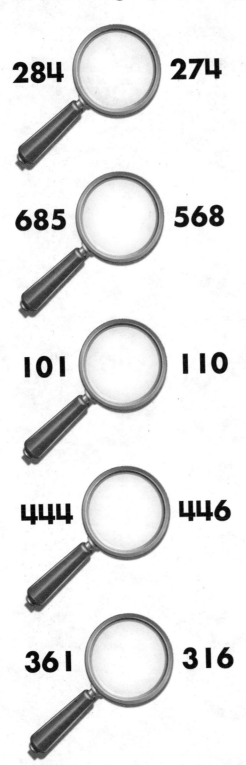

284 ◯ 274

685 ◯ 568

101 ◯ 110

444 ◯ 446

361 ◯ 316

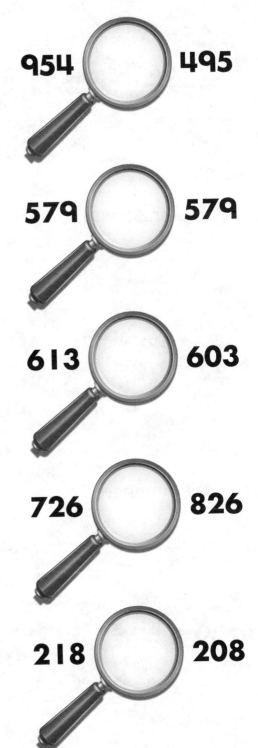

954 ◯ 495

579 ◯ 579

613 ◯ 603

726 ◯ 826

218 ◯ 208

Can You Compare?

Compare the numbers. Write >, <, or = in each magnifying glass.

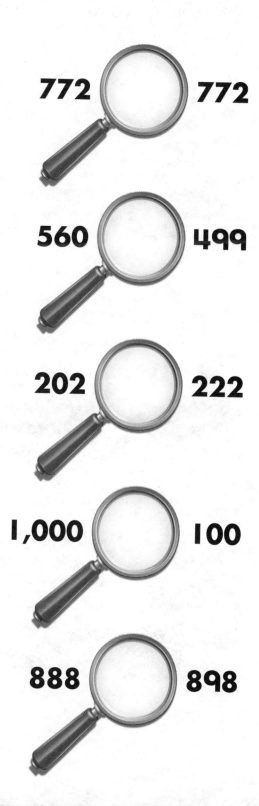

16 ◯ 106

399 ◯ 359

625 ◯ 652

450 ◯ 290

109 ◯ 190

772 ◯ 772

560 ◯ 499

202 ◯ 222

1,000 ◯ 100

888 ◯ 898

10 More

Yummy toppings are kept in jars at Smoothie Station. Look at the number on the first jar in each pair. On the second jar, write a number that is 10 more.

100 More

Look at the number on the first jar in each pair. On the second jar,
write a number that is 100 more.

What's Next?

Write the missing numbers to complete the pattern in each row.

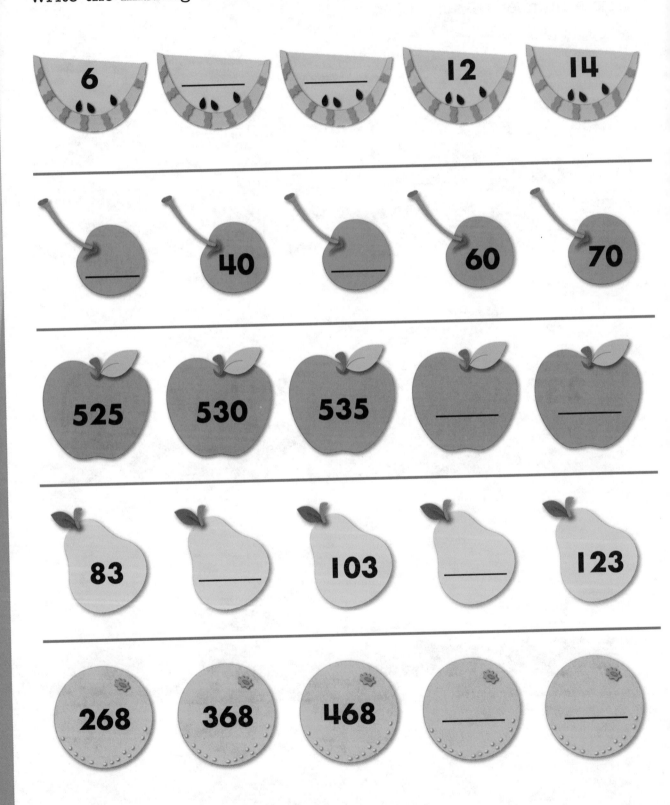

What's Next?

Write the missing numbers to complete the pattern in each row.

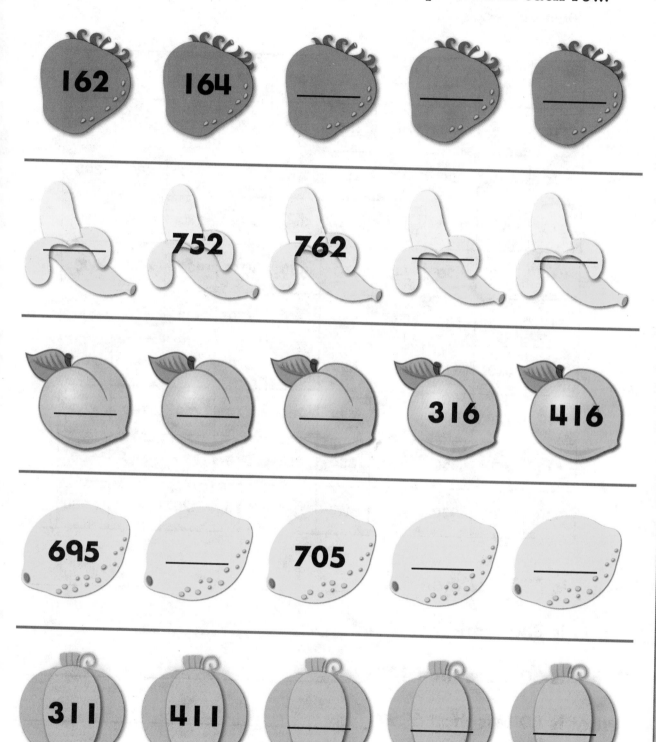

162   164   _____   _____   _____

_____   752   762   _____   _____

_____   _____   _____   316   416

695   _____   705   _____   _____

311   411   _____   _____   _____

One Thousand

The chart shows how to count to 1,000 by tens. Use it to answer the questions.

10	20	30	40	50	60	70	80	90	100
110	120	130	140	150	160	170	180	190	200
210	220	230	240	250	260	270	280	290	300
310	320	330	340	350	360	370	380	390	400
410	420	430	440	450	460	470	480	490	500
510	520	530	540	550	560	570	580	590	600
610	620	630	640	650	660	670	680	690	700
710	720	730	740	750	760	770	780	790	800
810	820	830	840	850	860	870	880	890	900
910	920	930	940	950	960	970	980	990	1,000

What is 200 less than 670? _____

What is 300 more than 530? _____

What is 30 more than 130? _____

What is 80 less than 690? _____

What is 500 more than 500? _____

Name

Rita's Readers

Add the numbers on each computer monitor to find out how many readers visited Rita's website that day. Regroup as needed.

38 16
75 50

Readers on Day #1: _____

59 15
82 46

Readers on Day #2: _____

90 50
60 45

Readers on Day #3: _____

26 88
47 19

Readers on Day #4: _____

62 79
85 93

Readers on Day #5: _____

12 28
64 51

Readers on Day #6: _____

Comment Count

It is time to collect more evidence about "The Mix-Up Mystery."

"Not only did lots of people read the blog post about the smoothie I made," Rita continued, "but lots of people left nice comments, too. They said that my smoothie creation sounded so creative and unusual. I think they all wanted to try it for themselves!"

"How many people left comments on your website?" asked Blenda Lott. To find the answer, add the numbers on each group of four mice.

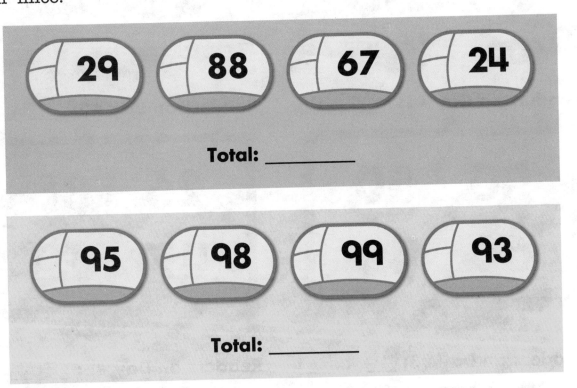

29   **88**   **67**   **24**

Total: _____

95   **98**   **99**   **93**

Total: _____

Use logic to decide which sum you wrote above belongs in the sentence below. Hint: Look back at the evidence you found on page 88 that tells how many people read Rita's blog post. Write your answer to complete the sentence.

Of the people who read Rita Ann Wright's blog post, _____ left comments.

You found evidence! Use the number you wrote to help you find a clue on page 106.

Hundreds and Hundreds

Solve the addition problems by adding all the hundreds, tens, and ones shown. Solve the subtraction problems by crossing out the hundreds, tens, and ones that are being taken away.

125 + 263 = _____

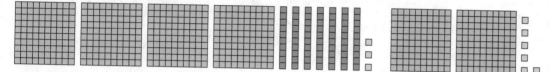

473 + 206 = _____

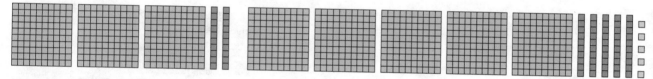

320 + 555 = _____

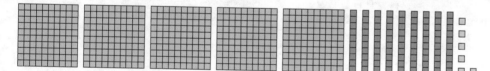

596 − 325 = _____

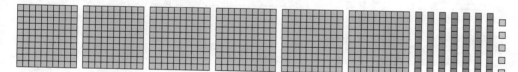

675 − 342 = _____

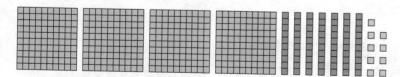

479 − 463 = _____

Regroup Tens and Hundreds

Add the ones, tens, and hundreds. Notice that the sum of the ones blocks is more than 10. Notice that the sum of the tens blocks is more than 100. Regroup by adding 1 ten to the tens column and 1 hundred to the hundreds column in each problem. The first one is done for you.

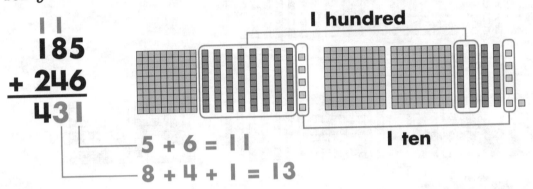

$$1\ 1$$
$$185$$
$$+\ 246$$
$$431$$

I hundred

I ten

5 + 6 = 11

8 + 4 + 1 = 13

276
+ 445

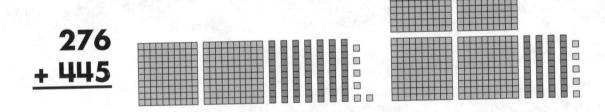

197
+ 346

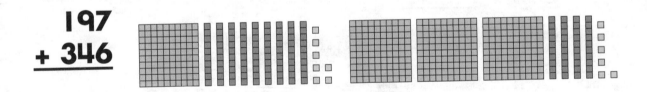

368
+ 153

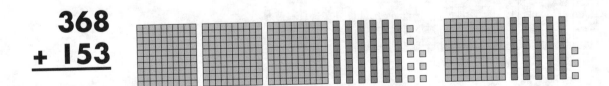

Regroup Tens and Hundreds

Subtract the ones, tens, and hundreds. Notice that there are not enough ones to subtract from. Notice that there are not enough tens to subtract from. Regroup 1 ten as 10 ones. Regroup 1 hundred as 10 tens. For each problem, draw the regrouped blocks. The first one is done for you.

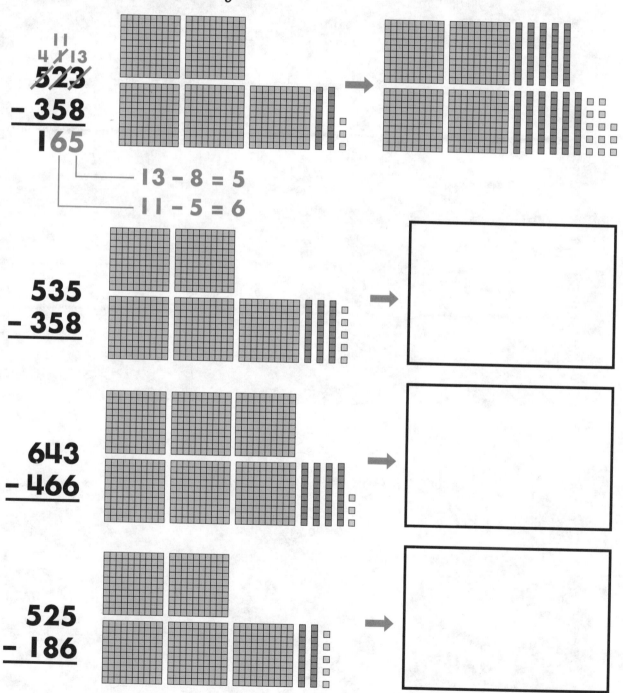

$$523 - 358 = 165$$

$$13 - 8 = 5$$
$$11 - 5 = 6$$

$$535 - 358$$

$$643 - 466$$

$$525 - 186$$

Delivery Day

Boxes of supplies were delivered to Smoothie Station. Choose numbers from the boxes to write in the blanks. Then, solve the problems you made!

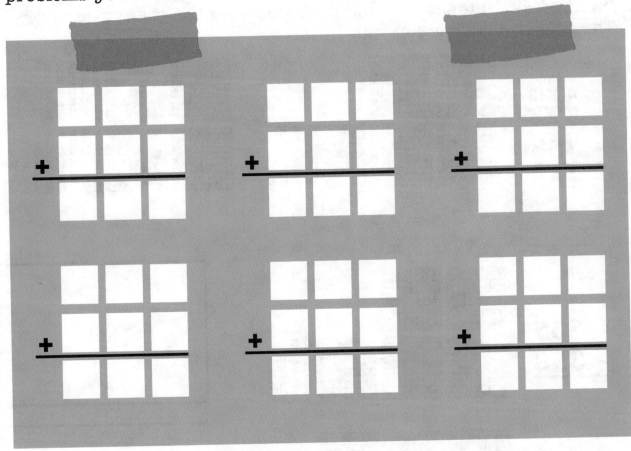

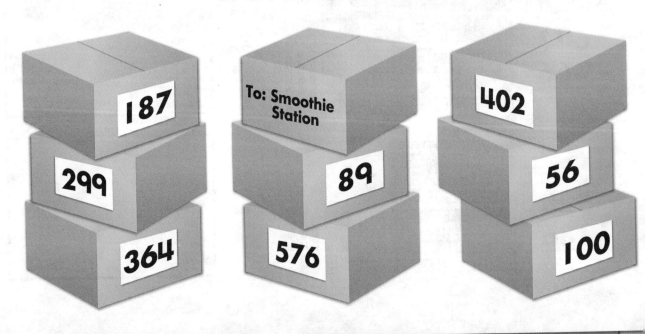

187

299

364

To: Smoothie Station

89

576

402

56

100

Delivery Day

Boxes of supplies were delivered to Smoothie Station. Choose numbers from the boxes to write in the blanks. Then, solve the problems you made!

688
105
754
52
951
99
136
357

What's the Problem?

Add or subtract. Regroup tens and hundreds as needed.

$$425 + 125$$

$$711 + 191$$

$$719 - 532$$

$$186 - 92$$

$$432 - 257$$

$$300 + 547$$

$$213 + 519$$

$$862 - 541$$

$$650 + 129$$

$$159 - 82$$

$$86 + 93$$

$$137 + 310$$

$$519 - 120$$

$$909 - 457$$

$$76 + 192$$

$$411 + 120$$

What's the Problem?

Add or subtract. Regroup tens and hundreds as needed.

$$312 + 85$$

$$186 - 107$$

$$543 - 206$$

$$720 + 140$$

$$546 - 121$$

$$714 + 251$$

$$252 + 130$$

$$259 - 147$$

$$456 - 291$$

$$612 + 319$$

$$591 + 120$$

$$132 - 41$$

$$683 - 419$$

$$540 - 75$$

$$712 + 163$$

$$312 + 105$$

Name

CLUE CORNER

Which Digit?

It is time to find a clue about "The Mix-Up Mystery"!

"You have a lot of readers!" exclaimed Blenda.

"I try to tell them all I can," said Ms. Wright. "In my blog post, I described how my smoothie looked, smelled, and tasted. I told everyone to come to Smoothie Station the very next day to try some delicious smoothies. I will tell even more in my big article."

"You told your readers to come the next day?" asked Blenda.

"Of course," replied Rita Ann Wright. "After all, it is my favorite thing to do." What is Ms. Wright's favorite thing? "To find out, write the numbers you collected as evidence on pages 68, 76, 88, and 98 to complete the problems.

Now, answer the questions. Write a letter in the box above each digit to finish the sentence and find a clue.

- What digit was subtracted from 4 hundreds? Write **a**.

- What digit appeared only in the ones and hundreds places? Write **r**.

- What digit means "no ones" or "no tens" in the problems? Write **s**.

- What digit was subtracted from 1 hundred regrouped as 10 tens? Write **e**.

- What digit appeared only in the sum and difference? Write **h**.

Clue: What is Rita Ann Wright's favorite thing to do?

Her favorite thing is to ☐ ☐ ☐ ☐ ☐ with readers.
                              0   2   3   4   8

Write the clue word you found in the Detective's Notebook on pages 202 and 203.

TOP SECRET FILE #3:
Grammar and Vocabulary

Learning Goals:

- Use collective nouns and reflexive pronouns
- Form irregular plural nouns
- Form the past tense of irregular verbs
- Choose between adjectives and adverbs
- Write and expand sentences
- Capitalize names of holidays, products, and places
- Use commas in greetings and closings
- Use context clues to understand word meanings
- Learn new vocabulary words
- Use prefixes, suffixes, and base words to build new words

Collect Evidence on These Evidence Alert! Pages:
Pages 116, 127, 137, 147

Use Evidence to Find a Clue on the Clue Corner Page:
Page 154

Clue Question:
Who did it?

Suspect:
Trudy Culors

The Whole Group

You use some collective nouns every day. A group of students is called a **class**. A group of spectators is called an **audience**. Some collective nouns are more unusual. Did you know that a group of chickens is called a **brood**? Draw lines to match the collective nouns with the groups they name.

a school of

a herd of

a pod of

a litter of

a swarm of

The Whole Group

Draw lines to match the collective nouns with the groups they name.

a flock of

a bunch of

a pride of

a colony of

an army of

Talking About Ourselves

Reflexive pronouns refer back to the noun that the sentence is talking about. They often end with **self** or **selves**. Circle a reflexive pronoun in each sentence. Draw an arrow from it back to the noun that it refers to.

The workers at Smoothie Station are proud of themselves.

Blenda's grandfather named the store himself.

You can help yourself to snacks.

I solved the mystery all by myself.

We made this recipe ourselves.

Trudy herself drew this picture.

Pick a Pronoun

Choose a reflexive pronoun to complete each sentence.

myself herself	himself themselves	yourself itself

Rita Ann Wright made this unusual smoothie

_____.

I _____ **love avocado-lime smoothies.**

The clumsy man spilled a drink on _____.

The workers at Smoothie Station clean up after

_____.

You can order from the menu for _____.

A purple pen was found all by _____.

Plurals Without s

Some plural nouns do not end with **s** or **es** or follow the rules you know. They are irregular plurals. Find each matching noun and plural noun. Color them with the same color.

feet

child

women

teeth

leaves

tooth

woman

foot

leaf

children

Plurals Without s

Find each matching noun and plural noun. Color them with the same color.

Pick a Plural

Circle the correct plural to complete each sentence.

A family with three (children/childs) waited in line for zoo tickets.

Four (mooses/moose) live in the North America section of the zoo.

These (womens/women) tell visitors about the giraffes.

Did you hear the (wolves/wolfs) howl?

Some (funguses/fungi) are growing under that tree.

Let's get French fried (potatoes/potatos) for lunch.

Pick a Plural

Circle the correct plural to complete each sentence.

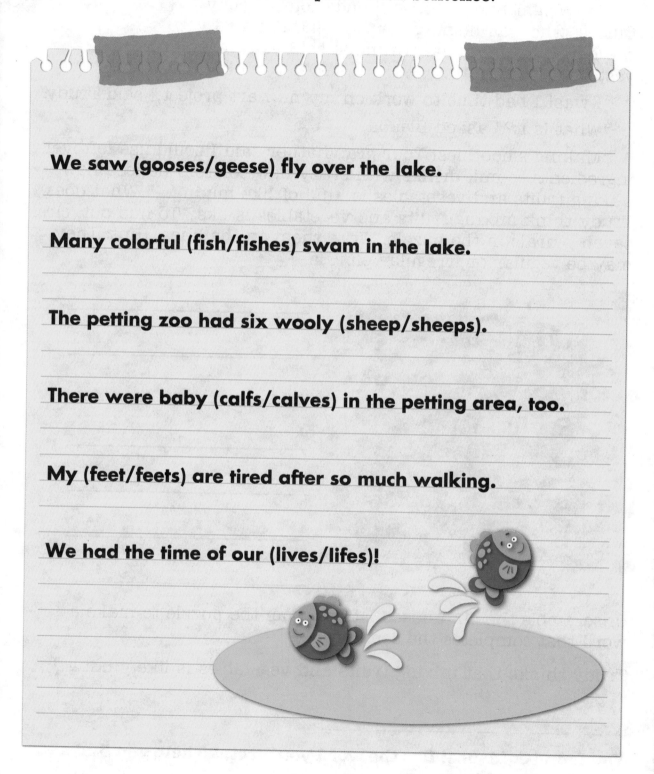

We saw (gooses/geese) fly over the lake.

Many colorful (fish/fishes) swam in the lake.

The petting zoo had six wooly (sheep/sheeps).

There were baby (calfs/calves) in the petting area, too.

My (feet/feets) are tired after so much walking.

We had the time of our (lives/lifes)!

Plurals and Projects

It is time to collect more evidence about "The Mix-Up Mystery."

Ms. Wright had to go, so Blenda found Trudy Culors, who was helping a customer. "I'm glad you are here!" said Blenda. "Grandpa said you were here yesterday, too."

"I was! I had time to work on my new art project," said Trudy.

"What is it?" asked Blenda.

"Making smoothies! Your grandfather said I could use leftover ingredients to mix drinks with crazy new colors. I noticed how mixing fruits and vegetables is kind of like mixing..." What does Trudy think mixing fruits and vegetables is like? To find out, circle seven plurals in the puzzle. Write them on the lines. Hint: They may be regular or irregular plurals.

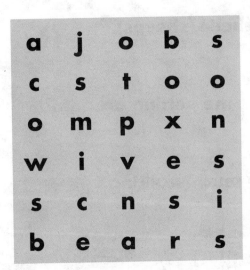

a	j	o	b	s
c	s	t	o	o
o	m	p	x	n
w	i	v	e	s
s	c	n	s	i
b	e	a	r	s

_____

_____

_____

_____

_____

_____

Unscramble the six unused letters from the puzzle to make a word that completes the sentence.

Trudy thinks that mixing fruits and vegetables is like mixing

____ ____ ____ ____ ____ ____.

You found evidence! Use the word you wrote to help you find a clue on page 154.

Evidence ALERT!

Irregular Verbs

Some verbs do not follow the patterns you know. Their past-tense forms do not end with **ed**. Use the verbs in the magnifying glasses to complete the sentences.

1. When Trudy has a thoughtful look on her face, she

   _____ probably thinking about her next art

   project.

2. Trudy and Blenda _____

   talking about what happened on Monday.

3. Blenda _____ not here when

   the mystery smoothies were made.

4. The customers at Smoothie Station _____

   unhappy that they could not order the new drink.

is
was
were

---

1. Blenda is _____ to solve the mystery.

2. Where did Rita Ann Wright _____?

3. Many customers _____ to

   Smoothie Station last weekend.

4. Trudy is _____ to mix fruits

   and vegetables.

go
going
went

Irregular Verbs

Some verbs do not follow the patterns you know. Their past-tense forms do not end with **ed**. Use the verbs in the magnifying glasses to complete the sentences.

1. Smoothies _____ many ingredients.

2. Blenda _____ been visiting her grandfather at work.

3. Trudy _____ lots of art supplies.

4. Yesterday, Blenda _____ a chocolate-coconut-banana smoothie.

have
has
had

1. Every day, Grandpa _____ many customers at his store.

2. Did anyone _____ who made the mystery smoothies?

3. Last week, Blenda _____ Trudy Culors after school every day.

4. How many people _____ Rita Ann Wright's blog post?

see
sees
saw

Irregular Verbs

Some verbs do not follow the patterns you know. Their past-tense forms do not end with **ed**. Use the verbs in the magnifying glasses to complete the sentences.

1. **Rita Ann Wright does not have time to cook, so she**

   _____ **at restaurants often.**

2. **Smoothie Station customers**

   _____ **50 granola bars**

   last week.

3. **Is it time to _____?**

4. **We _____ the last banana yesterday.**

eat

eats

ate

---

1. **Who _____ a purple pen on the table**

   yesterday?

2. **Rita Ann Wright had to**

   _____.

3. **Blenda comes to Smoothie Station after she**

   _____ **school.**

4. **Three customers just _____.**

leave

leaves

left

Irregular Verbs

Some verbs do not follow the patterns you know. Their past-tense forms do not end with **ed**. Use the verbs in the magnifying glasses to complete the sentences.

1. That customer always _____ a peach-mango

   smoothie.

2. Earlier today, a boy _____

   two gumballs.

3. A customer asked, "Can I

   _____ the same delicious smoothie I got

   yesterday?"

4. Last week, Trudy _____ new art supplies.

buy

buys

bought

---

1. What _____ Rita Ann Wright like to do?

2. _____ you think the mystery

   will be solved?

3. Trudy _____ not work last

   Sunday.

4. Blenda's grandfather _____ not come to the

   store on Mondays.

do

does

did

Name

Irregular Verbs

Some verbs do not follow the patterns you know. Their past-tense forms do not end with **ed**. Use the verbs in the magnifying glasses to complete the sentences.

1. Many people _____ to Smoothie Station to get

   a healthy snack.

2. What time was it when Trudy

   _____ to work?

3. Here _____ another customer.

4. Earlier, Blenda _____ into the back room and

   found evidence.

come

comes

came

---

1. Can you _____ some fresh strawberries?

2. This afternoon, Blenda _____ an

   unlatched window.

3. Blenda's grandfather often

   _____ ingredients at the

   farmer's market.

4. Has the answer to the puzzle been _____?

find

finds

found

It Describes a Noun

Adjectives describe nouns. Draw a line from each adjective to a noun that it could describe.

odorous

crunchy

light

blazing

cuddly

graceful

sun

skunk

popcorn

flamingo

teddy bear

balloon

It Describes a Verb

Adverbs describe verbs. They can tell how something happens. Many adverbs end with **ly**. Draw a line from each verb to an adverb that could describe it.

draw

runs

begs

sings

rattles

reads

hopefully

quietly

creatively

noisily

swiftly

joyfully

Adjective or Adverb?

Decide whether the underlined words are nouns or verbs. Then, choose adjectives or adverbs to describe them.

Adjectives	**Adverbs**
colorful	carefully
tiny	outside
excellent	often

1. Trudy Culors is an _____ <u>artist</u>.

2. She <u>draws</u> and <u>paints</u> _____.

3. Trudy has taken art classes since she was a

   _____ <u>girl</u>.

4. All of her <u>creations</u> are bright and _____.

5. Trudy <u>mixes</u> colors _____.

6. <u>Going</u> _____ always gives her new ideas for

   projects.

Adjective or Adverb?

Decide whether the underlined words are nouns or verbs. Then, choose adjectives or adverbs to describe them.

Adjectives	Adverbs
unusual	expertly
favorite	always
delicious	inside

1. Trudy likes <u>to work</u> _____ at Smoothie Station.

2. She thinks <u>smoothies</u> are _____ and fun to make.

3. She likes to use _____ <u>ingredients</u>.

4. Trudy _____ <u>mixes</u> up kiwis and carrots.

5. Some of her _____ <u>colors</u> are yellow, red, and orange.

6. Trudy _____ <u>smiles</u> at customers.

 +  **=**

New and Improved

Rewrite the sentences so that they tell more information. Choose adjectives and adverbs from the boxes to include in your new sentences.

Adjectives	Adverbs
fresh	quickly
sharp	tightly
creamy	slowly
tasty	carefully
whole	completely

1. Use limes and bananas to make this drink.

   _____

2. Chop the ice with a blade.

   _____

3. Squeeze the lime to collect its juice.

   _____

4. Pour in the juice.

   _____

5. Stir in the bananas.

   _____

6. Clean up the kitchen when you are done.

   _____

Which Color?

It is time to collect more evidence about "The Mix-Up Mystery."

As Trudy talked, Blenda observed the area where the older girl had been working. It was kind of messy. Puddles of juice and ice chips stood on the counter. Trudy's sketchbook lay open to a page covered in purple doodles. "Your project sounds really interesting," said Blenda. "What new colors did you make?"

"First," said Trudy, "I tried mixing grapes and lemons." What did Trudy call the color she made? To find out, complete the adjectives on purple crayons. Complete the adverbs on yellow crayons.

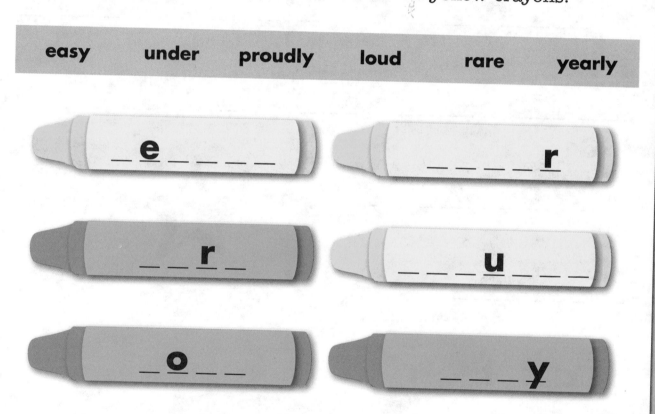

| easy | under | proudly | loud | rare | yearly |

_ **e** _ _ _ _   _ _ _ _ _ **r**

_ _ _ **r** _   _ _ _ _ **u** _ _ _

_ **o** _ _   _ _ _ **y**

Now, write the first letter of each word you wrote, in order from left to right, to form a made-up word that completes the sentence.

Trudy called her new color ____ ____ ____ ____ ____ ____.

You found evidence! Use the word you wrote to help you find a clue on page 154.

Capitals for Special Days

Important words in the names of holidays always begin with a capital letter. Write letters on the lines to complete the names of holidays. Use capital letters where they are needed.

_ hanks _ _ _ _ _ _ g _

_ hine e N _ _ _ _ ear

_ _ _ _ _ _ _ of _ uly

_ wa _ z _ _

_ _ _ bor _ ay

_ ast _ r

Name

Capitals for Special Days

Write letters on the lines to complete the names of holidays. Use capital letters where they are needed.

___ o l i ___

___ a m a ___ ___ n

___ l g ___ a y

___ ___ n u ___ k ___ h

___ a y of the ___ e ___ d

___ ___ ___ ___ w e e n

Capitals for Product Names

Important words in the names of products always begin with capital letters. Write a product name for each item.

Walk Right **Grandma's Homemade** **Stay Sharp**	**Fruit Fun** **Wake-Up Crunch** **Hold Tight**

cookies

jelly beans

cereal

shoes

paper clips

pencils

Capitals for Product Names

Write your own product name for each item. Make sure to begin each important word with a capital letter.

_____ **peanuts**

_____ **hats**

_____ **eggs**

_____ **yo-yos**

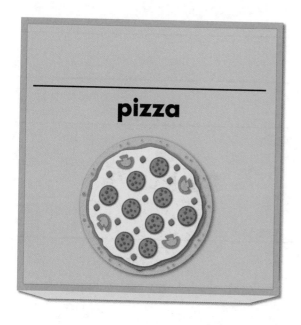

_____ **pizza**

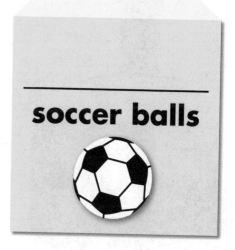

_____ **soccer balls**

Capitals for Place Names

Important words in the names of specific places begin with a capital letter. Write each place name under the category where it belongs.

Yellowstone National Park
Kansas City, Missouri
Willis Tower
Tampa, Florida
Acadia National Park

Liberty Bell
Golden Gate Bridge
New York, New York
Zion National Park

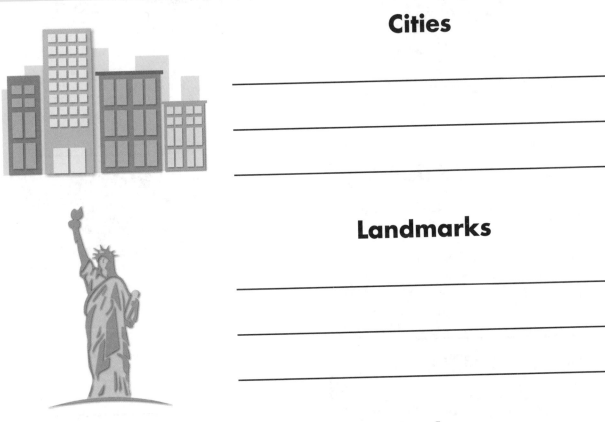

Cities

_____

_____

_____

Landmarks

_____

_____

_____

Parks

_____

_____

Name

Capitals for Place Names

For each category, write the names of places you know. Begin each important word with a capital letter.

Cities

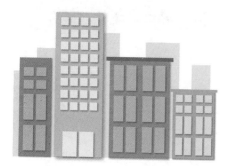

_____

_____

_____

_____

Landmarks

_____

_____

_____

_____

Parks

_____

_____

_____

_____

Take Note!

Proofread each note. Cross out each proofreading mark in the white box as you write it in the note.

Capitalize this letter. ≡	Add a comma. ∧	Add a period. ⊙

⊙ ∧ ∧ ≡ ≡ ≡

dear Mr Lott

    Thank you for talking to our class when we came to visit Smoothie station. We enjoyed learning all about your store. We especially liked the vanilla-berry smoothies you made for us. Come and visit us at school anytime!

Sincerely
northside Elementary School Room 212

⊙ ∧ ∧ ≡ ≡ ≡

dear Blenda

    I am glad you are helping solve the mystery at smoothie Station. i know you will find the answers I need I appreciate all your help around the shop. Let's have a yummy smoothie together soon!

Love
Grandpa

Name

Take Note!

Proofread each note. Cross out each proofreading mark in the white box as you write it in the note.

⊙ ⋀ ⋀ ≡ ≡ ≡

dear Rita ann Wright

I liked talking to you about your job. I like to tell stories with words and videos just like you do. Could I visit you at the newspaper office? Please let me know. I can't wait to read your article soon

sincerely
Blenda Lott

⊙ ⋀ ⋀ ≡ ≡ ≡

dear Mr. Tyler

I have some ideas for art projects at our school. One is to paint the fence outside in bright colors Another is to display bright pictures of fruits and vegetables in the cafeteria. I would like to help with these projects. Thank you for being a great art teacher!

your Student
Trudy culors

Dear Mr. Lott

Write a letter to the owner of Smoothie Station, Mr. Lott. Tell him about an idea you have for a new kind of smoothie. Explain what ingredients it will have and how it will taste. Use capital letters, commas, and punctuation correctly. Proofread your letter carefully.

Commas and Colors

It is time to collect more evidence about "The Mix-Up Mystery."

Trudy kept talking excitedly about her project. "Next," she explained to Blenda, "I tried another wild mix-up. I used cucumbers, kiwi fruits, honeydew melons, and blueberries. It was the most amazing color I have ever seen!" What did Trudy call the new color she made? To find out, read the names of places in the world whose names include colors. Insert four commas where they are needed. Circle five letters that should be capitals.

blue Mound Texas

Yellow Pine louisiana

emerald, Australia

White Cliffs of Dover, england

Orange California

Red Bank new Jersey

Now, write the letters you circled, in order, to find a made-up word that completes the sentence.

Trudy called the new color she made ____ ____ ____ ____ ____.

You found evidence! Use the word you wrote to help you find a clue on page 154.

Word Sleuth

Read the words in each magnifying glass that are related to each other. Use them to circle the best word to complete each sentence.

**pants
jacket
dress
blazer**

A blazer is something to

keep you cool.

wear.

button.

**boat
motorcycle
forklift
tractor**

A forklift is a type of

vehicle.

toy.

trip.

**oak
hickory
maple
pine**

A hickory is a type of

street.

flavor.

tree.

**wrench
hammer
screwdriver
pliers**

Pliers are

tools.

wood.

jobs.

Word Sleuth

Read the words in each magnifying glass that are related to each other. Use them to circle the best word to complete each sentence.

valley
mountain
riverbank
plateau

A plateau is a type of

water.

land.

map.

---

beetle
ant
mite
wasp

A mite is a type of

insect.

spider.

animal.

---

cheddar
cottage
Parmesan
Swiss

Parmesan is a type of

cheese.

food.

spice.

---

spoon
spatula
tongs
knife

A spatula is a type of

meal.

kitchen utensil.

food.

Where Does It Fit?

Write each word under the category it fits best.

magenta	cranberry	pineapple	fig
heat	blizzard	chop	whisk
raspberry	beige	hurricane	rain
thunderclap	combine	charcoal	violet

Weather Words

_____

_____

_____

_____

Fruits

_____

_____

_____

_____

Cooking Verbs

_____

_____

_____

Colors

_____

_____

_____

Where Does It Fit?

Write each word under the category it fits best.

gazelle	bank	price	savings
dictionary	elephant	watercolor	sketch
payment	easel	rhinoceros	thesaurus
paintbrush	atlas	encyclopedia	bonobo

Art Words

_____

_____

_____

_____

African Animals

_____

_____

_____

_____

Information Sources

_____

_____

_____

_____

Money Words

_____

_____

_____

_____

Context Clues

Look for clues in each sentence to help you circle the meaning of the colored word.

After paying for the smoothie, the customer asked for her receipt.

> money that is owed
>
> paper that tells how much was paid
>
> cash register

The store had too many bananas, and there was also a surplus of yogurt.

> too little
>
> the right amount
>
> too much

Since I don't like this one, can I exchange it for another kind?

> trade
>
> pay for
>
> throw away

At the price of only one dollar, that snack is a real bargain!

> something that is worthless
>
> a good deal
>
> something bought with a coupon

Please deposit the mop in the closet when you are done mopping.

> take out
>
> use
>
> put in

Name

Context Clues

Look for clues in each sentence to help you circle the meaning of the colored word.

I don't have enough money to buy it, so I asked Mom for a loan.

money earned

money borrowed

visit to a bank

The generous man bought smoothies for all 10 children in line.

unselfish

old

selfish

I chewed some gum, gave some to my sister, and put the balance in my room.

package

new

leftover amount

The medium smoothie costs one quarter less than the large one.

a half

a fourth

a lot

Can I have a discount on the price of this stale cookie?

amount subtracted

ten more

amount added

Shades of Meaning

Look at the words on each paint chip. Their meanings are similar, but not quite the same. Choose another word to write on each paint chip.

munch	run	pour	stare

peek

look

_____

trot

_____

sprint

drizzle

rain

_____

nibble

_____

gobble

Shades of Meaning

Choose another word to write on each paint chip.

| terrified | thrilled | stunning | tiptoed |

pretty

lovely

_____

_____

marched

strutted

scared

spooked

_____

joyful

_____

delighted

Shades of Meaning

Choose another word to write on each paint chip.

| strong | super | tiny | mystery |

puzzle

problem

_____

little

_____

miniature

_____

sturdy

everlasting

good

_____

amazing

Name _____

Mystery Meanings

Evidence ALERT!

It is time to collect more evidence about "The Mix-Up Mystery."

"You are talented at mixing new colors, and at making up funny names for them," Blenda told Trudy Culors.

"Thanks!" said Trudy. "I made the cucumber-kiwi-honeydew-blueberry smoothie on Monday morning. After I admired its awesome color, I made another discovery about it. Then, I had to tell everyone I know." How did Trudy let everyone know about the smoothie she made? To find out, write a word in the puzzle to match each meaning. Write the first letter of each word in the box with the matching number. Move around the square in a spiral.

1. someone who steals

2. just right

3. feeling alone

Begin at the bottom left corner and move clockwise. Write the letter you wrote in each corner of the puzzle, in order, to make a word that completes the sentence.

Trudy sent a ____ ____ ____ ____ about the smoothie to everyone she knows.

You found evidence! Use the word you wrote to help you find a clue on page 154.

Smooth Words

Combine each base word with the prefixes and suffixes shown. Write the new words on the lines. You may need to change the spelling of the base word.

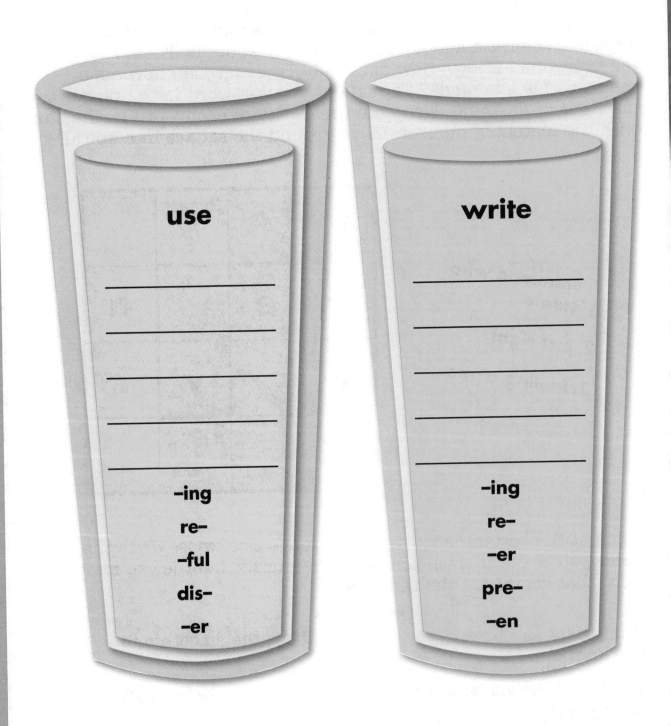

use

_____

_____

_____

_____

_____

–ing

re–

–ful

dis–

–er

write

_____

_____

_____

_____

_____

–ing

re–

–er

pre–

–en

Smooth Words

Combine each base word with the prefixes and suffixes shown. Write the new words on the lines. You may need to change the spelling of the base word.

lock

_____

_____

_____

_____

_____

–ing

un–

–er

re–

–ed

rest

_____

_____

_____

_____

_____

–ing

un–

–ful

–less

–ed

Write the Meaning

Use the prefix and suffix meanings to help you write a definition for each word.

dis = opposite of

er = one who

ness = state of

un or non = not

tion = act of

gardener = _____

dishonest = _____

addition = _____

nonfiction = _____

unhealthy = _____

illness = _____

Write the Meaning

Use the prefix and suffix meanings to help you write a definition for each word.

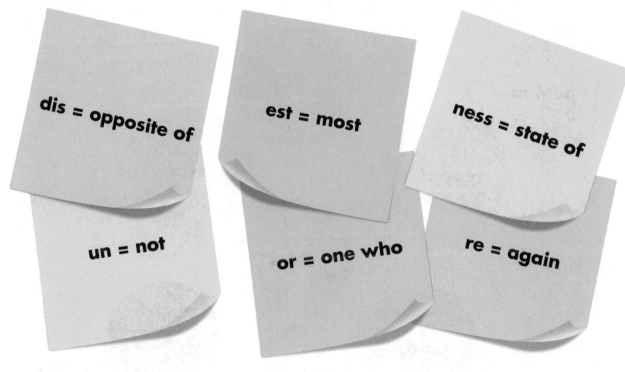

dis = opposite of

est = most

ness = state of

un = not

or = one who

re = again

collector = _____

reuse = _____

friendliest = _____

loudness = _____

dislike = _____

unhappy = _____

Base Word Balloons

Look at the words on each bunch of balloons. On the balloon weight, write the base word they share.

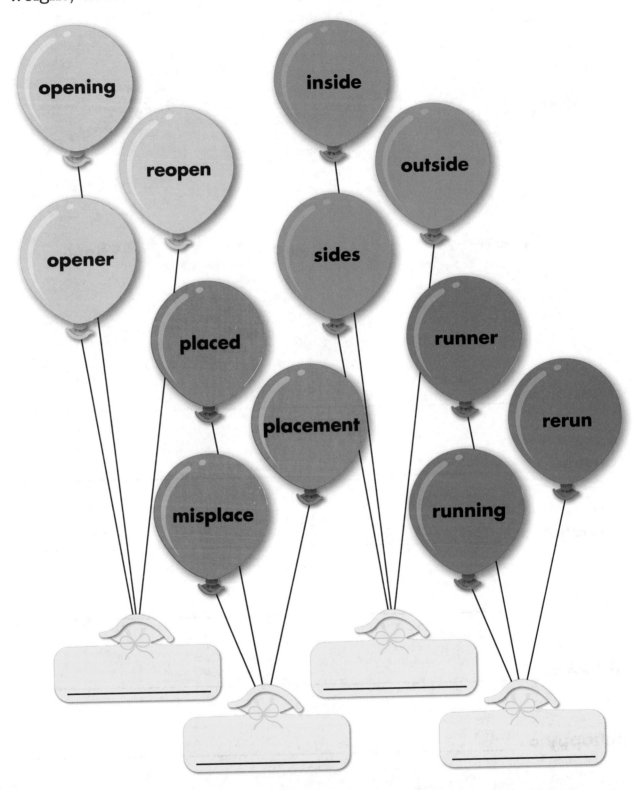

Base Word Balloons

Look at the words on each bunch of balloons. On the balloon weight, write the base word they share.

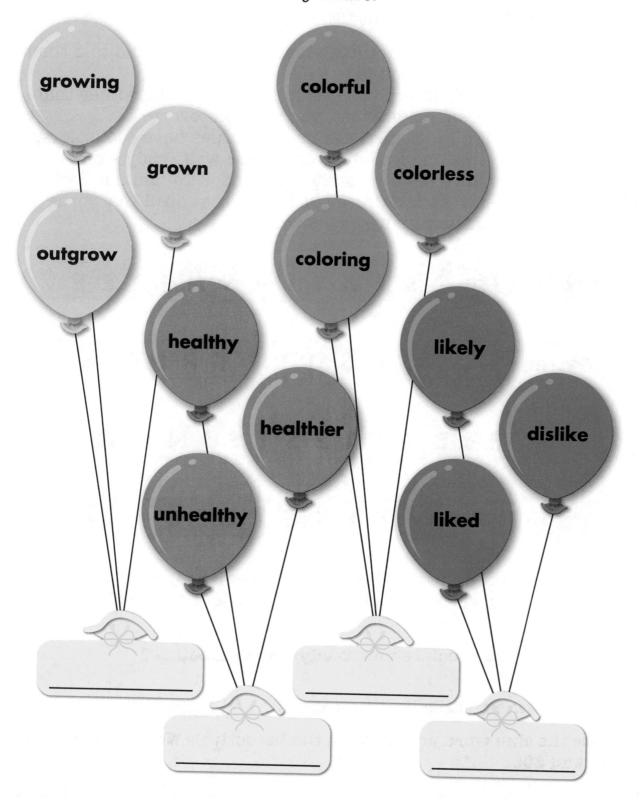

Slurp and See

It is time to find a clue about "The Mix-Up Mystery"!

"So, I texted everyone I know," continued Trudy, "and told them to come and try my smoothie."

"You said you discovered something," said Blenda, "other than the smoothie's great color. What was your discovery?"

"Well," said Trudy, "sometimes my smoothies have cool colors, but that is all. This one was different." How was Trudy's new smoothie different from others she has made? To find out, look at the letters on each straw. Cross out letters that spell the words you found as evidence on the pages shown.

Page 116: P R E A T I A S N T T E S

Page 127: Y T A S U T R Y P L E

Page 137: B T L A E S T E I N N G

Page 147: T E T A X S T T E D

Now, look at the words spelled by the letters you did not cross out. What base word do they all share? Write it to complete the sentence.

Clue: What was special about Trudy's new smoothie?

Trudy's new smoothie had a great color and a great _____.

Write the clue word you found in the Detective's Notebook on pages 202 and 203.

Name

TOP SECRET FILE #4:
Measurement, Time, Money, and Shapes

Learning Goals:

- Measure length in inches and centimeters
- Tell time to the nearest five minutes
- Count money
- Understand shapes
- Divide shapes into halves, thirds, and fourths
- Show data on line plots, bar graphs, and picture graphs

Collect Evidence on These Evidence Alert! Pages:
Pages 165, 175, 185, 195

Use Evidence to Find a Clue on the Clue Corner Page:
Page 201

Clue Question:
Who did it?

Suspect:
Brock Solid

Estimate It

Circle the unit of measurement that best measures each item.

car

inch   foot

notebook

inch   foot

dog

inch   foot

shoe

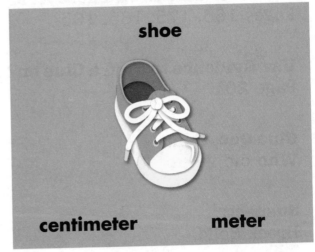

centimeter   meter

paper clip

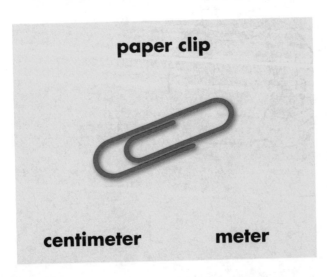

centimeter   meter

bee

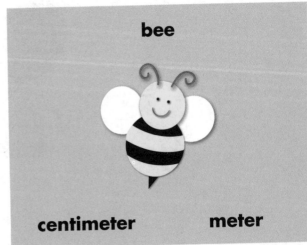

centimeter   meter

Estimate It

Circle the unit of measurement that best measures each item.

seashell

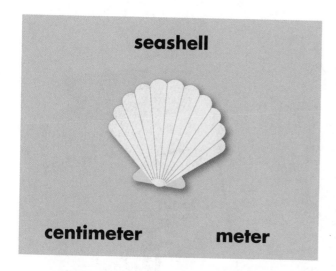

centimeter   meter

bathtub

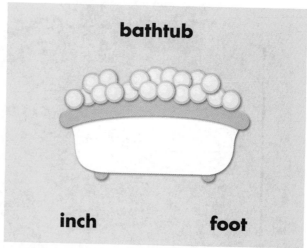

inch   foot

school bus

inch   foot

elephant

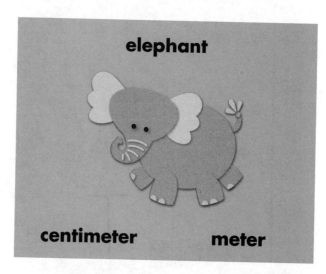

centimeter   meter

ant

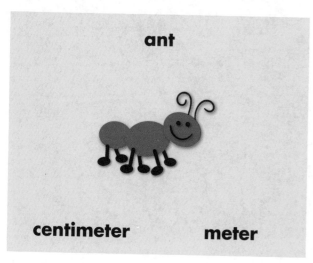

centimeter   meter

bed

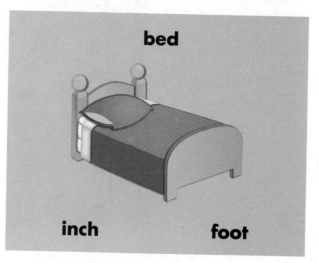

inch   foot

In Inches

Use a ruler to measure each animal in inches.

_____ inches

_____ inches

_____ inches

Name _____

In Centimeters

Use a ruler to measure each animal in centimeters.

_____ centimeters

_____ centimeters

_____ centimeters

Long and Heavy

Use a ruler to measure each barbell to the nearest inch. Then, measure each barbell again to the nearest centimeter. Answer the question.

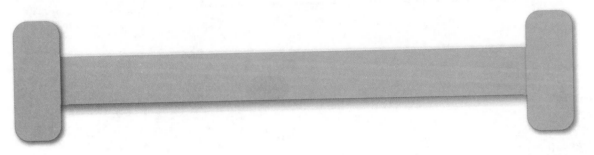

_____ inches   _____ centimeters

_____ inches   _____ centimeters

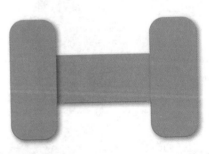

_____ inches   _____ centimeters

Which is longer, an inch or a centimeter? _____

Name

Long and Heavy

Use a ruler to measure each barbell to the nearest inch. Then, measure each barbell again to the nearest centimeter. Answer the question.

_____ inch   _____ centimeters

_____ inches   _____ centimeters

_____ inches   _____ centimeters

Which is shorter, an inch or a centimeter? _____

Measure Up!

Workers at Smoothie Station measured items from the shop in inches. Look at each item and its length.

5 inches

9 inches

5 inches

7 inches

10 inches

5 inches

9 inches

5 inches

$1

7 inches

9 inches

Measure Up!

Make a line plot to show the length of the items shown on page 162. For each item, draw **X** above its measurement in inches. Then, answer the questions.

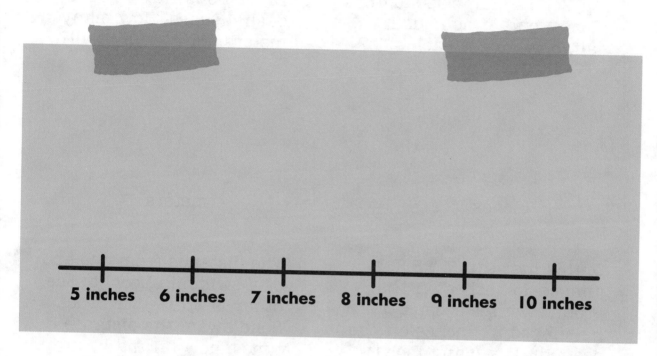

5 inches	6 inches	7 inches	8 inches	9 inches	10 inches

How many items are 5 inches long? _____ items

How many items are 8 inches long? _____ items

What is the total length of all items that are 9 inches long? _____ inches

What is the difference between the length of the shortest item and the length of the longest item? _____ inches

Measuring with Mr. Solid

Read and solve the story problems about Brock Solid's workouts.

Mr. Solid's jump rope is 48 inches long. If he folds it in half, how long is each side?

inches

Brock Solid ran a 100-meter dash 4 times. How many meters did he run in all?

meters

On his first try, Mr. Solid jumped 17 inches off the ground. On his second try, he jumped 21 inches off the ground. How many inches did he jump in all?

inches

The distance from one end of a swimming pool to the other is 26 feet. If Brock Solid swam the distance 3 times, how far did he swim?

feet

On Saturday, Mr. Solid biked 17 miles. On Sunday, he biked 12 miles. How many miles in all did he bike that weekend?

miles

Brock Solid's 5-pound hand weights are 18 centimeters long. His 8-pound hand weights are 25 centimeters long. How much longer are the 8-pound hand weights?

centimeters

Inch-Up

Evidence ALERT!

It is time to collect more evidence about "The Mix-Up Mystery."

Just then, Brock Solid came into the shop, whistling. He was so tall and his shoulders were so wide that he nearly filled up the doorway. "Howdy!" he said cheerfully.

"Mr. Solid!" exclaimed Blenda. "I was hoping you'd be here today."

"I try to come every afternoon right after my workout," he explained. "You will never guess how many chin-ups I did today!" How many chin-ups did Brock Solid do? To find out, use a ruler to measure each bar to the nearest inch.

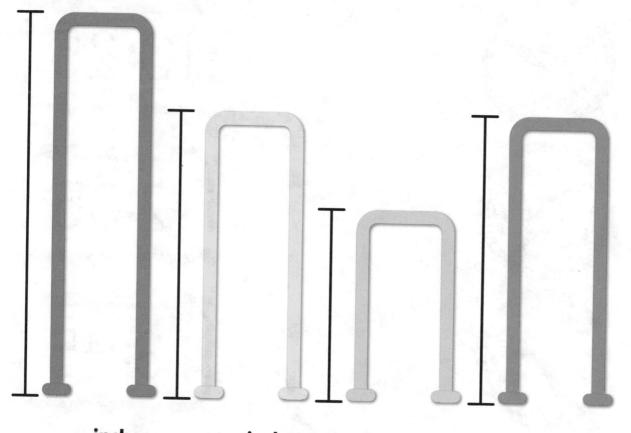

_____ inches   _____ inches   _____ inches   _____ inches

Add all the inches you measured above. Write the sum to complete the sentence.

Brock Solid did _____ chin-ups.

You found evidence! Use the number you wrote to help you find a clue on page 201.

Two Ways to Tell Time

Draw a line to match each clock face to a digital time.

5:55

10:25

2:35

3:45

12:10

Name

Two Ways to Tell Time

Draw a line to match each clock face to a digital time.

6:20

7:30

1:40

4:15

11:05

What Time Is It?

Look at the time on each clock face. Write the same time on each digital clock.

What Time Is It?

Look at the time on each clock face. Write the same time on each digital clock.

The Hands of Time

Look at the time shown on each digital clock. Draw hands on the clock face to show the same time.

The Hands of Time

Look at the time shown on each digital clock. Draw hands on the clock face to show the same time.

Time and Time Again

Read each time. Show it on two different kinds of clocks.

five o'clock

three thirty

quarter after one

quarter to six

seven o'clock

five minutes after two

Name

Time and Time Again

Read each time. Show it on two different kinds of clocks.

quarter to five
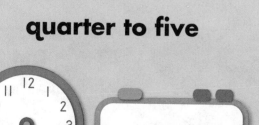

quarter after two

five minutes after one

eight o'clock

four thirty

half past nine

Beginnings and Endings

Read each story problem. Draw hands on the first clock to show the start time. Draw hands on the second clock to show the end time.

Start   **End**

 Brock Solid started his workout at ten o'clock. He finished one hour and fifteen minutes later. What time did his workout end?

Start   **End**

 On Monday, Mr. Solid got to Smoothie Station at 1:15. He worked on a new healthy smoothie recipe for 30 minutes. What time did he finish?

Start   **End**

Brock Solid left Smoothie Station at five o'clock. It took him twenty minutes to drive home. Then, he walked his dog for thirty minutes. What time did he finish walking his dog?

Name

Clock Path

It is time to collect more evidence about
"The Mix-Up Mystery."

"Have you been working on any new healthy
recipes?" Blenda asked Brock Solid.

"You betcha! I have one here," Mr. Solid said as he
pulled from his pocket a crumpled paper covered in green ink.
"This smoothie is packed with super-healthy ingredients. It has
pumpkin, soy milk, honey, and scoops of flax seeds." How many
scoops of flax seeds were in the new recipe? To find out, find a
pattern in the times shown on the clocks. Trace a path through the
maze.

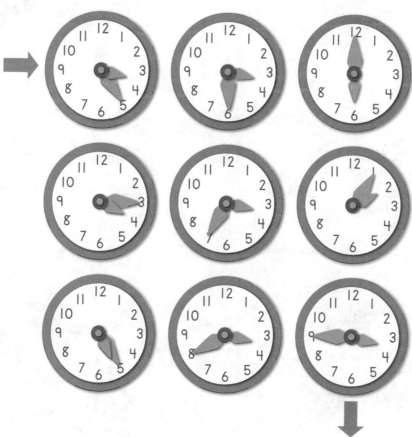

How many minutes were added to each clock in the pattern? Write
the number to complete the sentence.

Brock Solid's recipe had _____ scoops of flax seeds.

**You found evidence! Use the number you wrote to help you find a
clue on page 201.**

Pennies and Nickels

Write the amount shown by the coins.

5¢ 1¢ 5¢

_____ ¢

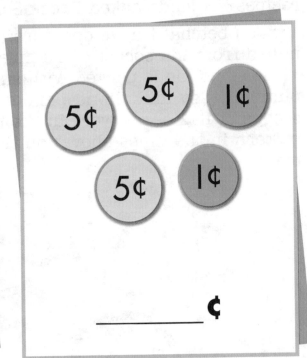

5¢ 5¢ 1¢ 5¢ 1¢

_____ ¢

1¢ 5¢ 1¢

_____ ¢

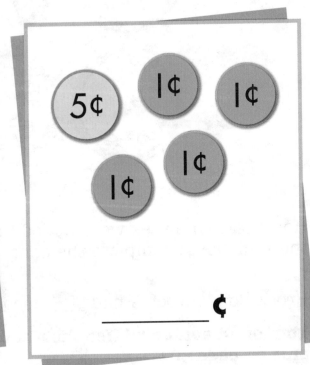

5¢ 1¢ 1¢ 1¢ 1¢

_____ ¢

Pennies, Nickels, and Dimes

Write the amount shown by the coins.

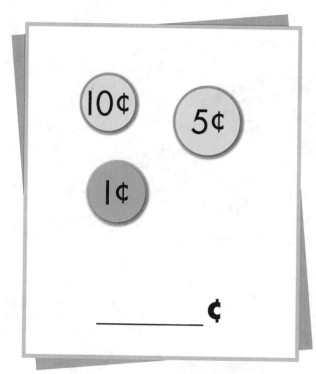

_____ ¢

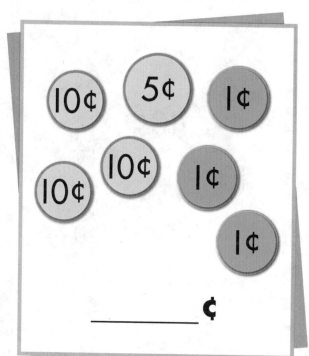

_____ ¢

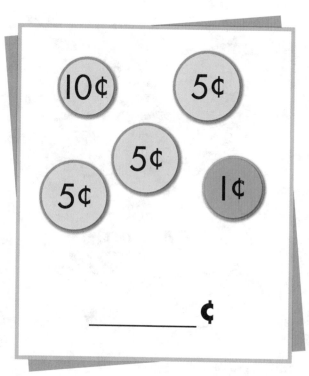

_____ ¢

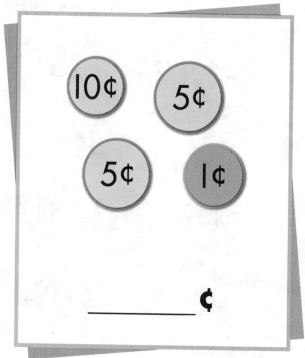

_____ ¢

Name _____

Pennies, Nickels, Dimes, and Quarters

Write the amount shown by the coins.

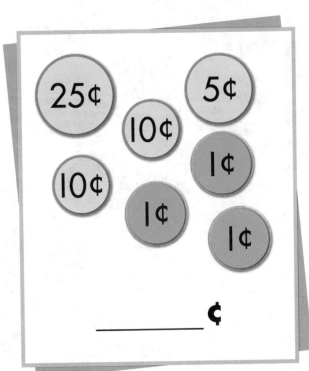

25¢ 5¢ 10¢ 1¢ 10¢ 1¢ 1¢

_____ ¢

25¢ 10¢ 5¢ 25¢ 5¢ 5¢

_____ ¢

25¢ 25¢ 25¢ 5¢ 5¢ 5¢ 1¢ 1¢ 5¢ 1¢ 1¢

_____ ¢

25¢ 10¢ 10¢ 25¢ 5¢ 10¢ 5¢ 1¢

_____ ¢

Name

Coins and Dollar Bills

Write the amount shown by the coins and bills.

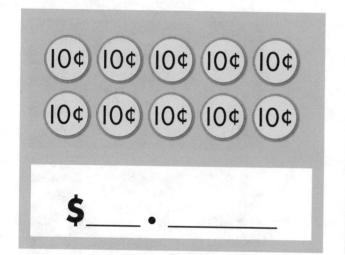

$_____ . _____

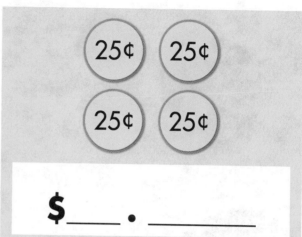

$_____ . _____

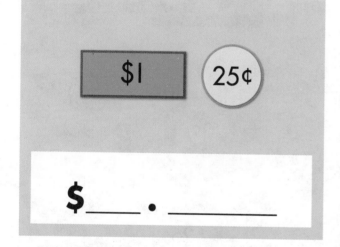

$_____ . _____

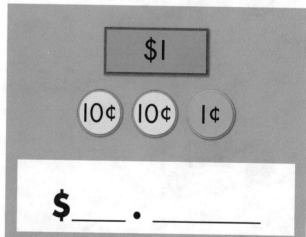

$_____ . _____

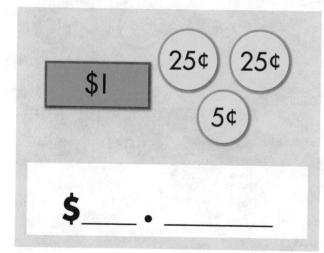

$_____ . _____

$_____ . _____

How Much?

Draw a line from each toy to the amount of money it costs.

36¢

68¢

43¢

57¢

22¢

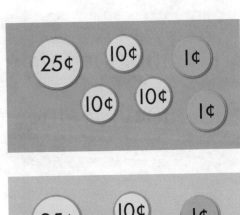

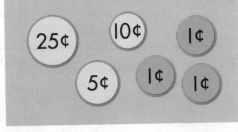

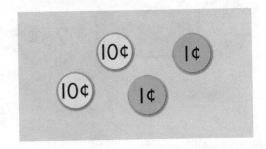

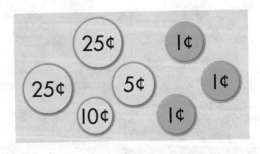

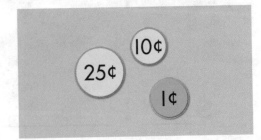

How Much?

Draw a line from each food item to the amount of money it costs.

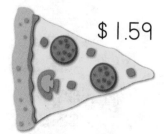 $1.59

 $.77

 $1.95

 $1.27

 $.89

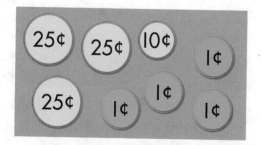

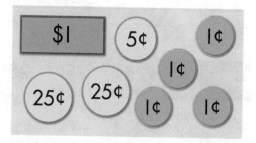

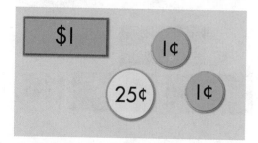

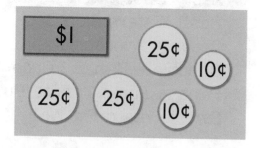

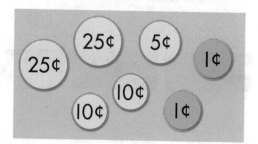

What's Your Order?

Read the menu. Write the name of the smoothie you could buy with each amount shown.

Smoothie Station Menu

Cherry Berry Oat Blast	$2.79
Carrot Citrus Spice Splash	$3.29
Zesty Chocolate Almond Orange	$2.58
Basil Watermelon Cooler	$4.09
Creamy Avocado Banana	$3.49
Chocolate Banana Coconut	$1.99
Papaya Pomegranate Punch	$4.36
Sweet Potato Fig Walnut	$3.99

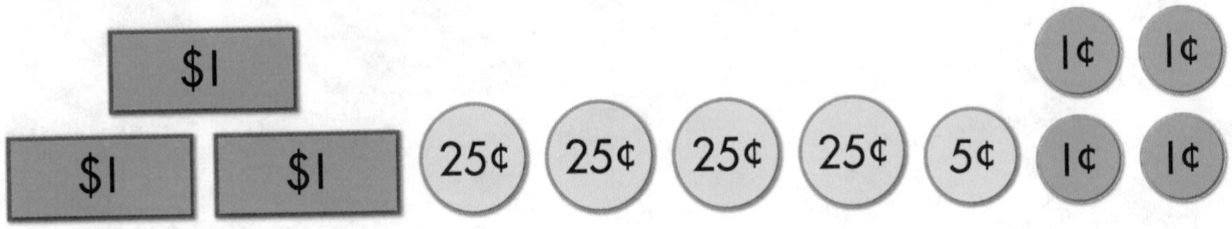

$1 $1 $1   25¢ 25¢ 25¢ 25¢ 5¢ 1¢ 1¢ 1¢ 1¢

_____

$1   25¢ 25¢ 25¢ 10¢ 10¢ 1¢ 1¢ 1¢ 1¢

_____

$1 $1 $1   25¢ 1¢ 1¢ 1¢ 1¢

_____

What's Your Order?

Read the menu. Write the name of the smoothie you could buy with each amount shown.

Smoothie Station Menu

Chocolate Raspberry Delight $4.25
Tropical Pineapple Mango Orange $3.72
Blueberry Lemon Chiller. $2.55
Chocolate Pepper Pear $3.59
Pea Raisin Papaya Surprise. $4.60
Tomato Melon Cilantro Zinger $3.75
Smooth Vanilla Berry Banana $4.15
Nutty Grape Guava. $3.29

$1

$1 10¢ 10¢ 10¢ 10¢ 10¢ 1¢ 1¢ 1¢ 1¢ 1¢

$1 $1 25¢ 25¢ 25¢ 25¢ 25¢ 25¢ 25¢

$1

$1 $1 25¢ 25¢ 25¢ 10¢ 10¢ 10¢ 10¢

Coin Sort

Get a handful of coins. Place them on the graph to show how many of each coin you have. Write the total amount at the bottom of each column.

Totals: _____ ¢ _____ ¢ _____ ¢ $_____ . _____ _____

Smoothie Cents

It is time to collect more evidence about "The Mix-Up Mystery."

"Flax seed is good for your heart and helps prevent disease," explained Brock Solid. "It has healthy oils, vitamins, and fiber."

"So a flax seed smoothie is good for you, but does it taste good?" Blenda asked.

"That is what I wondered," said Mr. Solid. "A few days ago, I mixed up a batch and asked eight people to try it. Guess how many thought that it tasted scrump-diddly-icious." How many people liked the smoothie? To find out, circle four groups of bills and coins that equal one hundred cents.

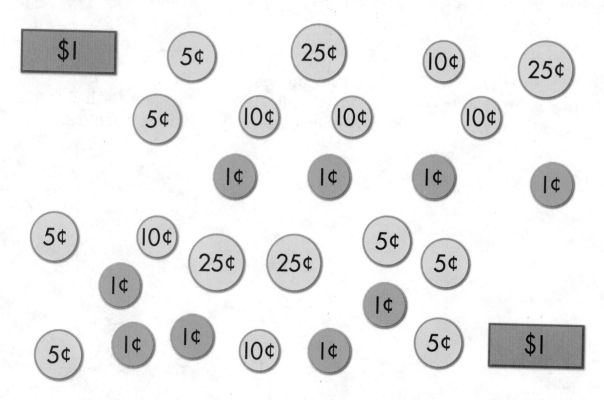

Count the money that you did not circle. Write the number of cents to complete the sentence.

Eight people tried the flax seed smoothie, and _____ liked it.

You found evidence! Use the number you wrote to help you find a clue on page 201.

I Am a Shape

Write the name of a shape to complete each sentence. Then, follow the directions to draw more shapes.

I have 0 sides and 0 corners. I am a

_____.

Draw two more shapes with 0 sides and 0 corners.

I have 3 sides and 3 corners. I am a

_____.

Draw two more shapes with 3 sides and 3 corners.

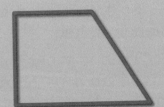

I have 4 sides and 4 corners. I am a

_____.

Draw two more shapes with 4 sides and 4 corners.

I Am a Shape

Write the name of a shape to complete each sentence. Then, follow the directions to draw more shapes.

I have 5 sides and 5 corners. I am a

_____.

Draw two more shapes with 5 sides and 5 corners.

I have 6 sides and 6 corners. I am a

_____.

Draw two more shapes with 6 sides and 6 corners.

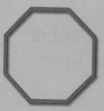

I have 8 sides and 8 corners. I am an

_____.

Draw two more shapes with 8 sides and 8 corners.

Angles, Faces, and Sides

Circle the shapes that match the descriptions. You may circle more than one shape in each row.

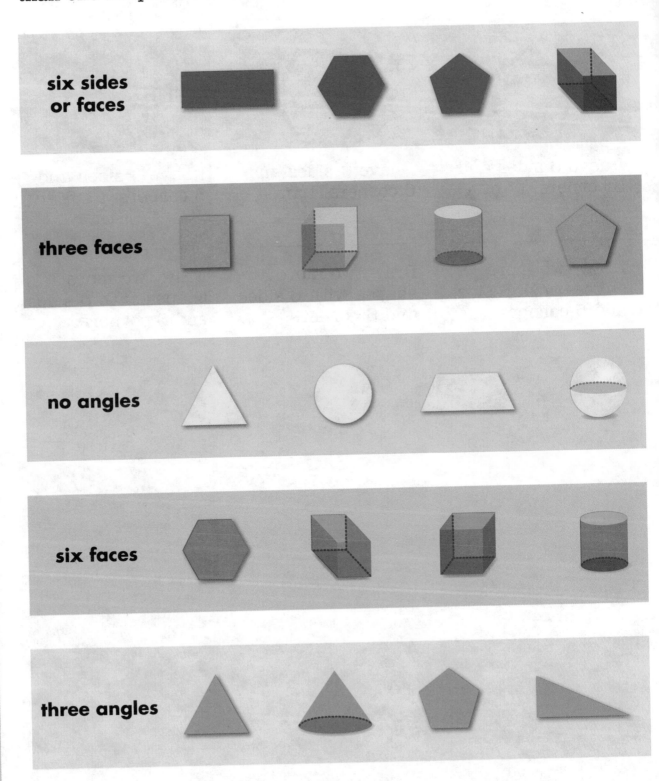

six sides or faces

three faces

no angles

six faces

three angles

Stack and Roll

Decide if each figure will roll, stack, or do both. Circle your answers.

roll **stack**

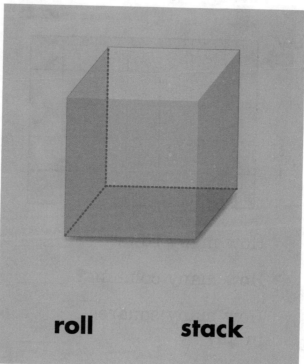

roll **stack**

roll **stack**

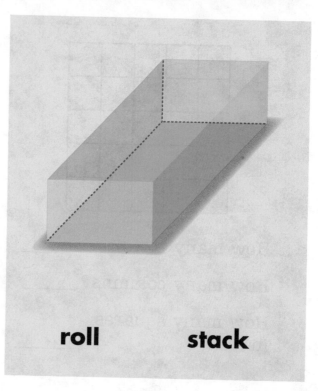

roll **stack**

How Many Squares?

Answer the questions about each divided shape.

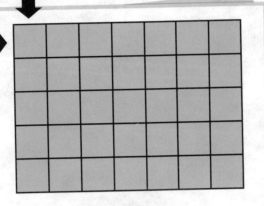

How many rows? _____

How many columns? _____

How many squares
in all? _____

How many rows? _____

How many columns? _____

How many squares
in all? _____

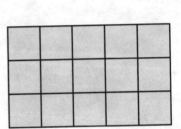

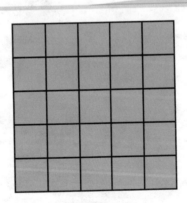

How many rows? _____

How many columns? _____

How many squares
in all? _____

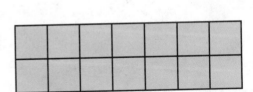

How many rows? _____

How many columns? _____

How many squares
in all? _____

How Many Squares?

Draw lines down and across to divide each shape into the number of rows and columns shown. Then, count the squares you made to answer the question.

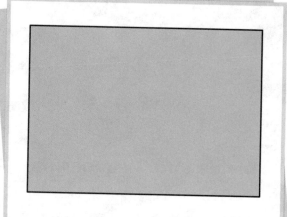

Make 4 rows and 5 columns.

How many squares in all? _____

Make 4 rows and 4 columns.

How many squares in all? _____

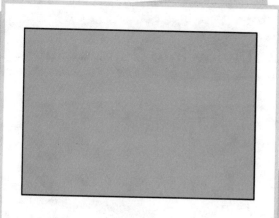

Make 7 rows and 3 columns.

How many squares in all? _____

Make 3 rows and 3 columns.

How many squares in all? _____

Equal Shares

Draw lines to divide each food item into equal shares.

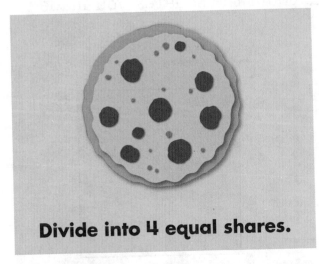

Divide into 4 equal shares.

Divide into 2 equal shares.

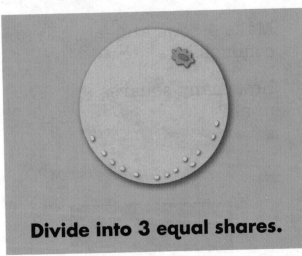

Divide into 3 equal shares.

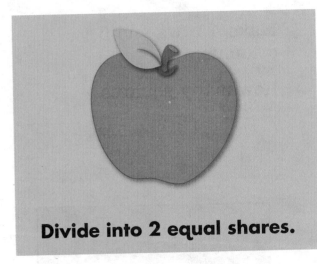

Divide into 2 equal shares.

Divide into 4 equal shares.

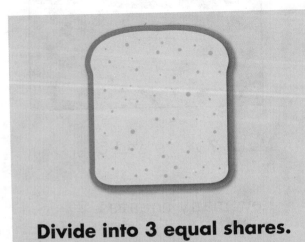

Divide into 3 equal shares.

Name

Equal Shares

Draw lines to divide each food item into equal shares.

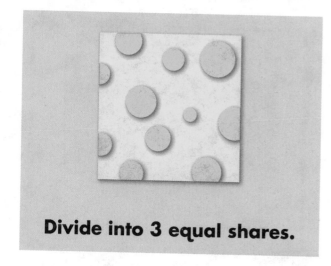

Divide into 3 equal shares.

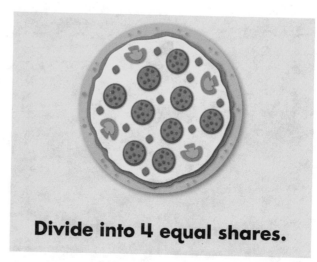

Divide into 4 equal shares.

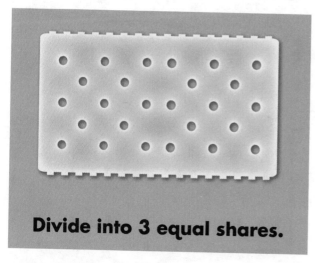

Divide into 3 equal shares.

Divide into 2 equal shares.

Divide into 2 equal shares.

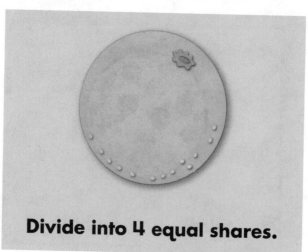

Divide into 4 equal shares.

How Much Is Left?

Circle the label that best describes each portion of the food that is left.

fourth   **half**

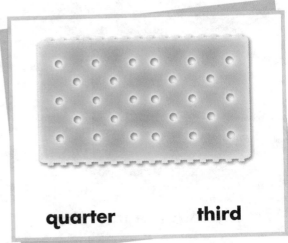

quarter   **third**

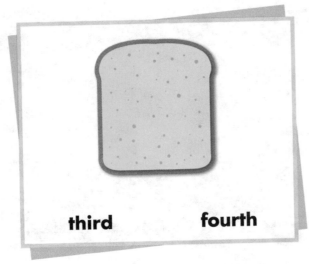

third   **fourth**

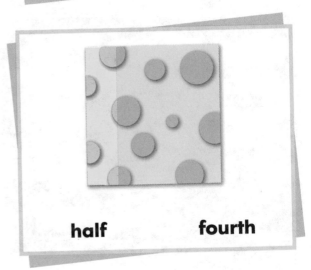

half   **fourth**

third   **half**

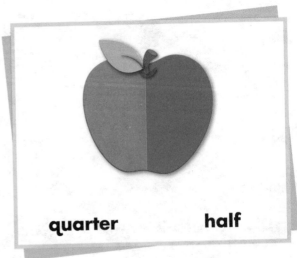

quarter   **half**

Quarters in Order

It is time to collect more evidence about "The Mix-Up Mystery."

"Do you often ask customers to try new recipes?" Blenda asked Brock Solid.

"Sure do! Just yesterday, I mixed up something especially healthy and nutritious. I invited everyone to try it." Mr. Solid was standing near the back-room door. As he spoke, Blenda noticed that he nervously flipped the window latch up and down.

"How many people tried your new smoothie yesterday?" wondered Blenda. To find the answer to Blenda's question, color fourths to complete the patterns.

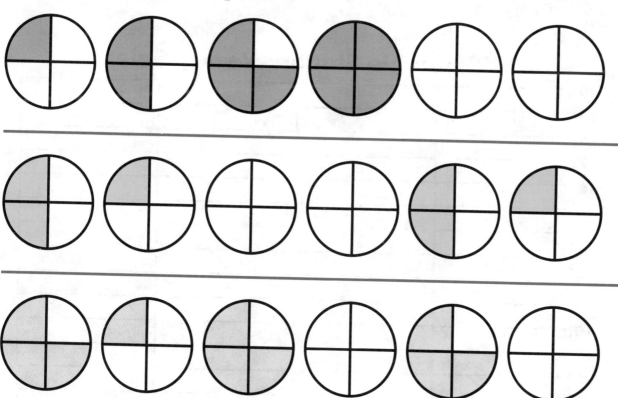

How many fourths did you color in all? Write the number to complete the sentence.

Yesterday, _____ customers tried Brock Solid's healthy new smoothie.

You found evidence! Use the number you wrote to help you find a clue on page 201.

Smoothie Sales

Look at Mr. Lott's notes about how many different types of smoothies were sold this week. Color in the bar graph to show the information.

Chocolate Banana Coconut: 卌 |||

Vanilla Berry Blast: 卌 卌 卌 |

Mint Cooler: 卌 卌 |||

Carrot Citrus Splash: 卌 卌 |||

Smoothie Station Weekly Sales

	Chocolate Banana Coconut	Vanilla Berry Blast	Mint Cooler	Carrot Citrus Splash
20				
19				
18				
17				
16				
15				
14				
13				
12				
11				
10				
9				
8				
7				
6				
5				
4				
3				
2				
1				
0				

Name

Smoothie Sales

Look at Mr. Lott's notes about how many different types of smoothies were sold this week. Color in the bar graph to show the information.

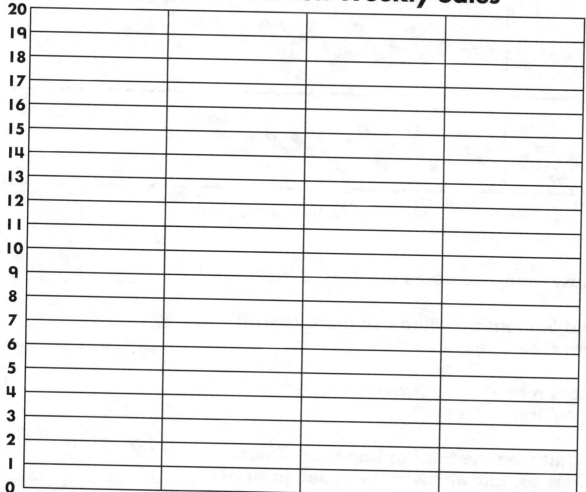

Creamy Vanilla: 𝍤𝍤 𝍤𝍤 𝍤𝍤

Apricot Zinger: 𝍤𝍤 𝍤 𝍤

Lemon Honey Spice: 𝍤 ||||

Sweet Potato Sipper: 𝍤𝍤 𝍤𝍤

Smoothie Station Weekly Sales

	Creamy Vanilla	Apricot Zinger	Lemon Honey Spice	Sweet Potato Sipper
20				
19				
18				
17				
16				
15				
14				
13				
12				
11				
10				
9				
8				
7				
6				
5				
4				
3				
2				
1				
0				

Fruit Graph

Read the graph that shows how many pieces of fruit were used at Smoothie Station in April. Use it to answer the questions.

Fruit Used in April

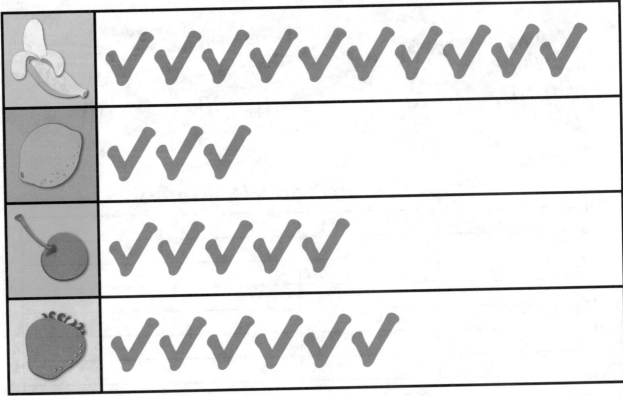

✔ = 10 pieces of fruit

How many bananas were used in April? _____

Did Smoothie Station use more cherries
or more limes in April? _____

How many more strawberries were
used than limes? _____

What was the total of bananas, limes,
cherries, and strawberries used in April? _____

Fruit Graph

Read the graph that shows how many pieces of fruit were used at Smoothie Station in May. Use it to answer the questions.

Fruit Used in May

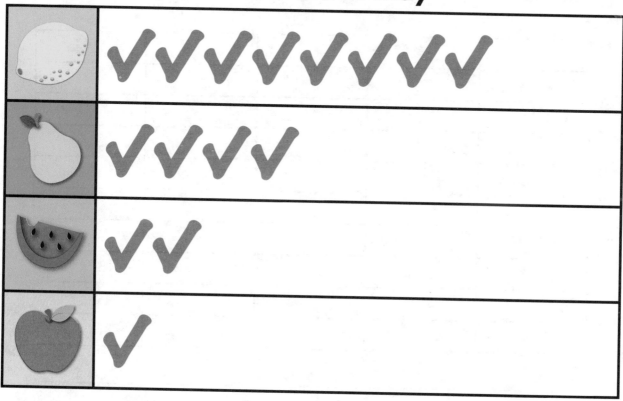

✔ = 10 pieces of fruit

How many pears and apples were used in May? _____

How many more lemons were used than watermelons? _____

Were more watermelons or apples used in May? _____

What was the total of lemons, pears, watermelons, and apples used in May? _____

Graph It!

Ask 10 people to name their favorite flavor of smoothie or ice cream. Write the names of the flavors they named at the bottom of each column in the graph. Then, color a bar to show how many people liked that flavor. Use your graph to answer the questions.

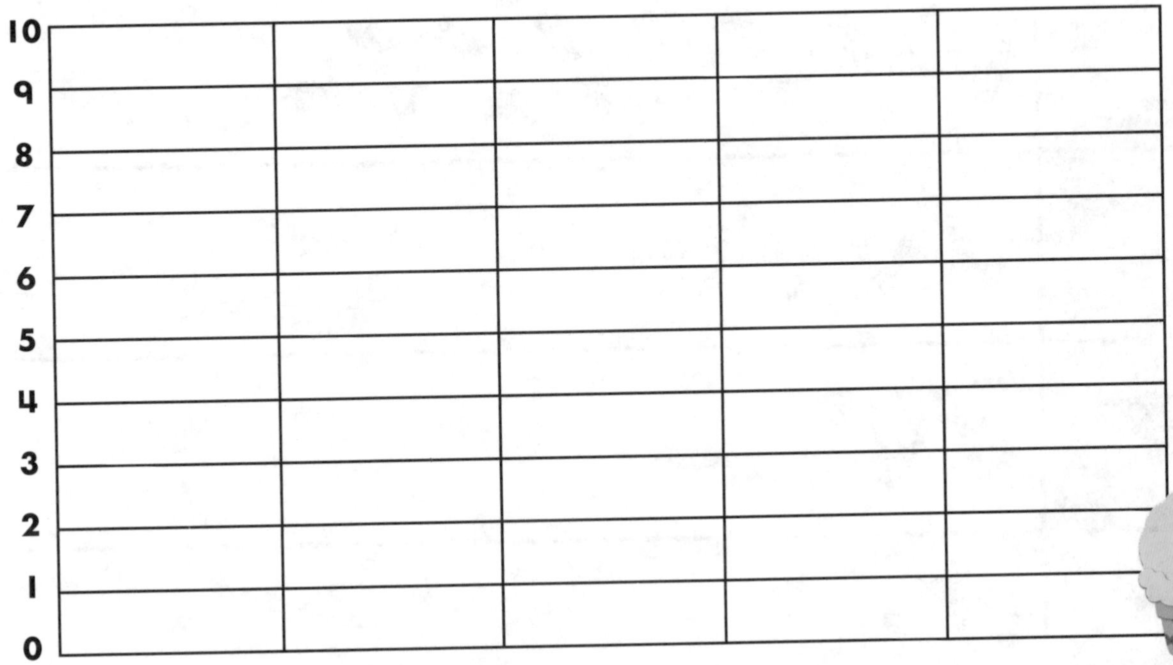

10					
9					
8					
7					
6					
5					
4					
3					
2					
1					
0					

_____ _____ _____ _____ _____

_____ _____ _____ _____ _____

What was the favorite flavor? _____

What was the least favorite flavor? _____

What was the difference between the most favorite and the least

favorite flavor? _____

What is your favorite flavor? _____

_____

Super Grapher

It is time to find a clue about "The Mix-Up Mystery"!

"Mighty sorry you weren't here yesterday, Blenda," continued Brock Solid, "to taste my latest smoothie recipe. I think your grandfather should put it on the menu right away. It has fruit and a super-healthy ingredient packed with vitamins and fiber that helps digestion and blood flow!" Mr. Solid was getting very excited. He accidentally knocked over a cup of apple juice that puddled on the floor. "I wish everyone loved to drink such healthy smoothies!"

"What is this super ingredient?" asked Blenda. To find the answer, graph the numbers you collected as evidence on the pages shown below.

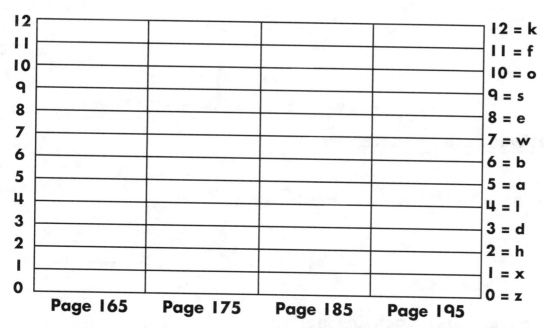

Look at each bar you made on the graph. Write the letters for the bars, in order, to make a word that completes the sentence.

Clue: What super-healthy ingredient is in Brock Solid's new recipe?

Brock Solid's new smoothie recipe has ____ ____ ____ ____.

Write the clue word you found in the Detective's Notebook on pages 202 and 203.

THE MIX-UP MYSTERY Detective's Notebook

When were the mystery smoothies sold?
(See page 8.)

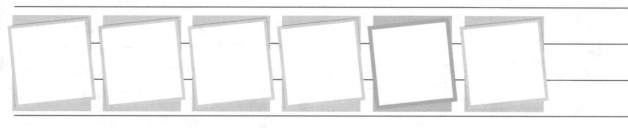

What was in the smoothies?
(See page 8.)

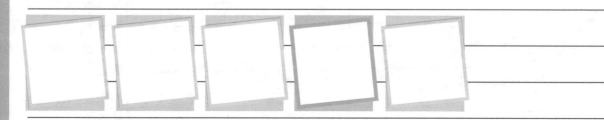

Where were the smoothies made?
(See page 58.)

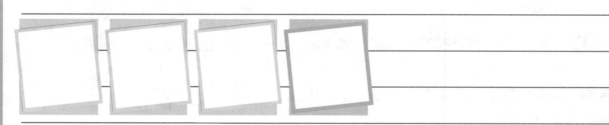

THE
MIX-UP
MYSTERY
Detective's
Notebook

Who DID IT?

Rita Ann Wright: What is her favorite thing to do?
(See page 106.)

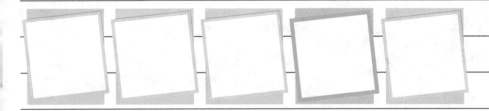

Trudy Culors: What was special about her new smoothie?
(See page 154.)

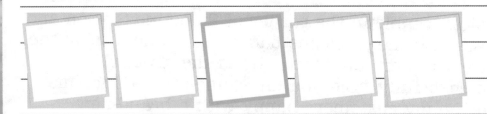

Brock Solid: What super-healthy ingredient is in his new

recipe? (See page 201.)

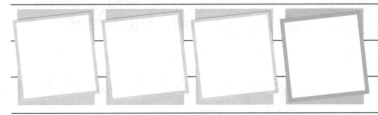

You have collected all the clues. Now, use the letters in green boxes in your **Detective's Notebook** in order. Circle those letters in the story choices below. Then, read the ending to the mystery. You did it, second grade investigator! You solved the case!

The Mix-Up Mystery, conclusion

Blenda Lott sat at a table in the corner of Smoothie Station and reviewed her notes. Did the clues she had gathered help solve the mystery? Just then, her grandfather entered the shop. "There's my girl!" he said cheerfully. "Did you find some answers for me? I would love to make my customers happy with a brand-new delicious smoothie."

"Grandpa, I think someone was mixing smoothies in the back of the store yesterday," Blenda began. "The window on the back-room door was unlatched. And a customer walked up to the window expecting to get served there."

A. "Hmm," said Mr. Lott. "That is strange. I always make sure that window is latched tight."

B. "Nothing to worry about," said Mr. Lott. "Mr. Solid is always playing with that latch."

C. "Smoothies could not be made in the back," said Mr. Lott. "All the blenders are in the front of the shop."

"Then, when I explored the back," continued Blenda, "I found seeds and a sticky mess on the floor."

H. "That could not be a mess from yesterday," said Mr. Lott. "I cleaned up the back room myself last night."

I. "Maybe it was so busy yesterday," Mr. Lott reasoned, "that the back room did not get cleaned up. Did you say seeds? What could those be from?"

J. "Smoothie Station should always be spic and span!" exclaimed Mr. Lott. "I will remind everyone to clean up!"

"Rita Ann Wright might have made the mystery smoothies," suggested Blenda. "She loved the smoothie you helped her make on Sunday. She posted a story and a video about it. She told everyone to come and try it."

K. "I don't think so," said Mr. Lott. "Ms. Wright does not know how to cook at all! I tasted the smoothie she made. It was awful!"

L. "That might be it," said Mr. Lott. "Do you have any other ideas?"

M. "Good work," said Mr. Lott. "That must be it! I will ask Rita for her recipe right away."

"It could be Brock Solid," offered Blenda. "He is always inventing healthy recipes. And he invites customers to try them."

P. "That might be it," said Mr. Lott. "Do you have any other ideas?"

Q. "Good work," said Mr. Lott. "Brock said he was working on something fantastic. We will put it on the menu right away!"

R. "That could not be it," said Mr. Lott. "His new kale recipe is healthy, but it is not very tasty. It needs a lot of work."

"Maybe it was Trudy," tried Blenda. "You said she could use leftover ingredients to blend new colors. Yesterday, by accident, she made a cucumber-fruit smoothie that looked and tasted great. She told people to come try it."

S. "Good work," said Mr. Lott. "That must be it! Cucumbers you say? I'll speak to Trudy right away."

T. "That might be it," said Mr. Lott. "Do you have any other ideas?"

U. "That could not be it," said Mr. Lott. "Trudy is just a kid. She could not invent a delicious smoothie."

"Trudy is very creative, but I found out she is not the only creative one around here," said Blenda. "It seems that everyone loves to blend new kinds of smoothies."

D. "We can't have everyone making crazy creations and messing up the shop!" cried Mr. Lott.

E. "That is true," said Mr. Lott. "After the new smoothie is on the menu, we should have a contest to see who else can make something yummy and unique!"

F. "We have enough smoothies on the menu at Smoothie Station," said Mr. Lott. "There is no room for more."

"I know we will have lots of new customers after Rita Ann Wright's article comes out," said Mr. Lott. "I am so glad we will have new smoothies to offer them. You are a clever investigator, Blenda Lott. Thanks for solving the mystery at Smoothie Station!"

"You are welcome, Grandpa," said Blenda. "Let me know the next time there is a case to crack!"

A Consonant Begins It

Write a beginning consonant letter for each word. Color the pictures.

h_orse	j_ellyfish	g_oat
c_at	z_ebra	l_adybug
q_uestion	y_o-yo	t_urtle
v_est	w_orm	s_cissors

Page 10

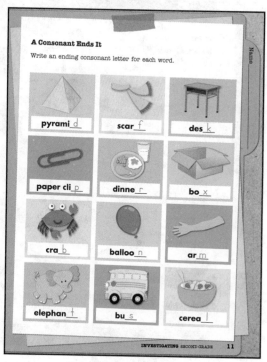

A Consonant Ends It

Write an ending consonant letter for each word.

pyrami_d	scar_f	des_k
paper cli_p	dinne_r	bo_x
cra_b	balloo_n	ar_m
elephan_t	bu_s	cerea_l

Page 11

Consonant Blends and Teams

Choose a consonant blend or team from the magnifying glass to complete each word.

gr fl
sk cl
th fr
br cr

sk_ate
fl_amingo
br_ush
cl_ock
fr_og
mou_th
cr_ab
gr_apes

Page 12

Consonant Blends and Teams

Choose a consonant blend or team from the magnifying glass to complete each word.

ch ng
sn tr
st sh
wh pl

sn_ail
st_ar
pea_ch
pl_um
ri_ng
tr_ash
wh_ale
sh_ell

Page 13

Page 14

Page 15

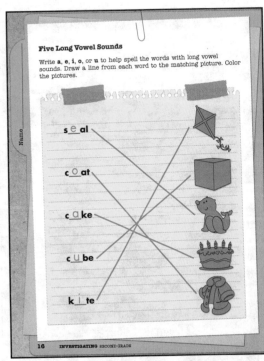

Page 16

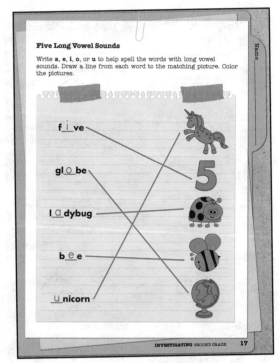

Page 17

Page 18

Page 19

Page 20

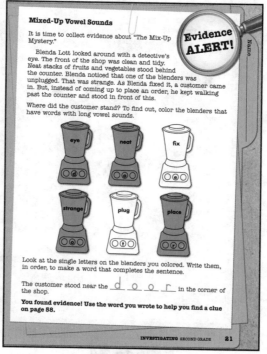

Page 21

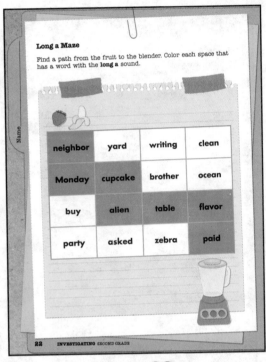

Long a Maze

Find a path from the fruit to the blender. Color each space that has a word with the **long a** sound.

neighbor	yard	writing	clean
Monday	cupcake	brother	ocean
buy	alien	table	flavor
party	asked	zebra	paid

22 INVESTIGATING SECOND GRADE

Page 22

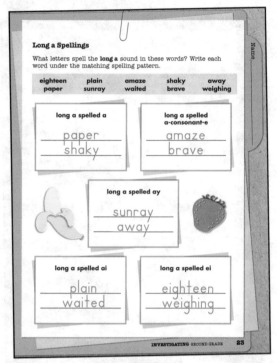

Long a Spellings

What letters spell the **long a** sound in these words? Write each word under the matching spelling pattern.

eighteen	plain	amaze	shaky	away
paper	sunray	waited	brave	weighing

long a spelled a
paper
shaky

long a spelled a-consonant-e
amaze
brave

long a spelled ay
sunray
away

long a spelled ai
plain
waited

long a spelled ei
eighteen
weighing

INVESTIGATING SECOND GRADE 23

Page 23

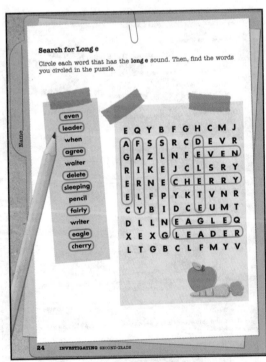

Search for Long e

Circle each word that has the **long e** sound. Then, find the words you circled in the puzzle.

even
leader
when
agree
waiter
delete
sleeping
pencil
fairly
writer
eagle
cherry

```
E Q Y B F G H C M J
A F S S R C D E V R
G A Z L N F E V E N
R I K E J C L S R Y
E R N E C H E R R Y
E L F P Y K T V N R
C Y B I D C E U M T
D L L N E A G L E Q
X E X G L E A D E R
L T G B C L F M Y V
```

24 INVESTIGATING SECOND GRADE

Page 24

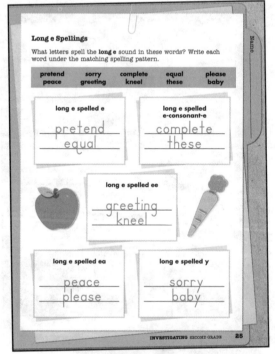

Long e Spellings

What letters spell the **long e** sound in these words? Write each word under the matching spelling pattern.

pretend	sorry	complete	equal	please
peace	greeting	kneel	these	baby

long e spelled e
pretend
equal

long e spelled e-consonant-e
complete
these

long e spelled ee
greeting
kneel

long e spelled ea
peace
please

long e spelled y
sorry
baby

INVESTIGATING SECOND GRADE 25

Page 25

ANSWER KEY

Page 26

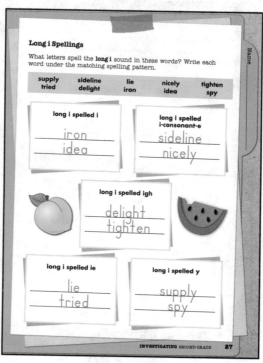

Page 27

Page 28

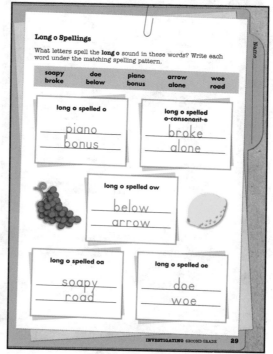

Page 29

INVESTIGATING SECOND GRADE   **211**

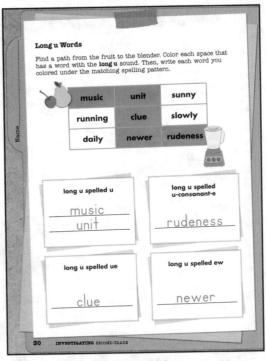

Page 30

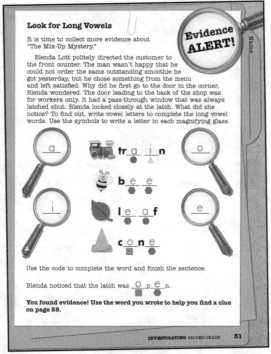

Page 31

Page 32

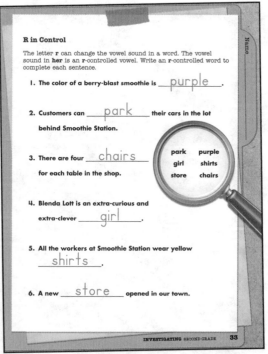

Page 33

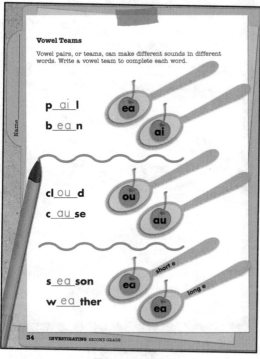

Page 34

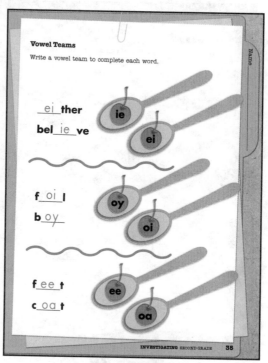

Page 35

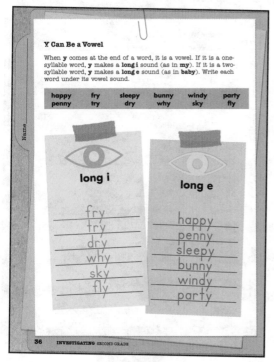

Page 36

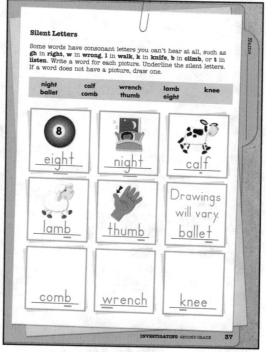

Page 37

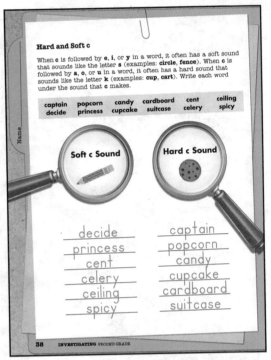

Page 38

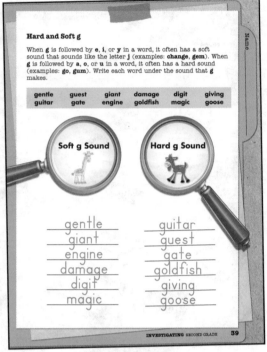

Page 39

Page 40

Page 41

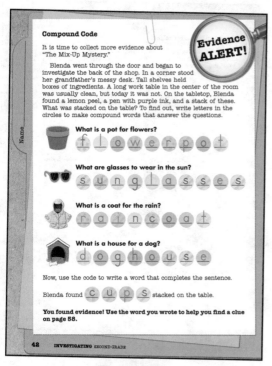

Compound Code

It is time to collect more evidence about "The Mix-Up Mystery."

Blenda went through the door and began to investigate the back of the shop. In a corner stood her grandfather's messy desk. Tall shelves held boxes of ingredients. A long work table in the center of the room was usually clean, but today it was not. On the tabletop, Blenda found a lemon peel, a pen with purple ink, and a stack of these. What was stacked on the table? To find out, write letters in the circles to make compound words that answer the questions.

Evidence ALERT!

What is a pot for flowers?
f l o w e r p o t

What are glasses to wear in the sun?
s u n g l a s s e s

What is a coat for the rain?
r a i n c o a t

What is a house for a dog?
d o g h o u s e

Now, use the code to write a word that completes the sentence.

Blenda found c u p s stacked on the table.

You found evidence! Use the word you wrote to help you find a clue on page 58.

42 INVESTIGATING SECOND GRADE

Page 42

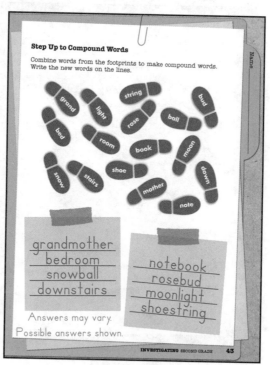

Step Up to Compound Words

Combine words from the footprints to make compound words. Write the new words on the lines.

grandmother
bedroom
snowball
downstairs

notebook
rosebud
moonlight
shoestring

Answers may vary.
Possible answers shown.

INVESTIGATING SECOND GRADE 43

Page 43

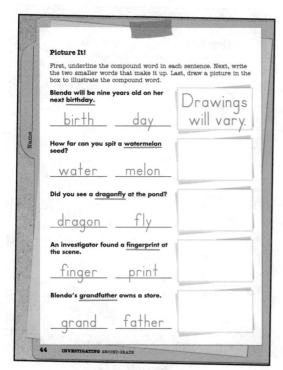

Picture It!

First, underline the compound word in each sentence. Next, write the two smaller words that make it up. Last, draw a picture in the box to illustrate the compound word.

Blenda will be nine years old on her next birthday.
birth   day

Drawings will vary.

How far can you spit a watermelon seed?
water   melon

Did you see a dragonfly at the pond?
dragon   fly

An investigator found a fingerprint at the scene.
finger   print

Blenda's grandfather owns a store.
grand   father

44 INVESTIGATING SECOND GRADE

Page 44

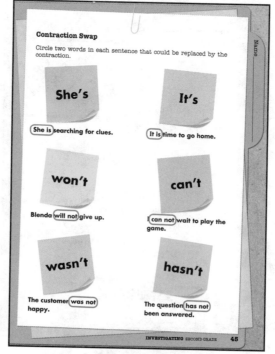

Contraction Swap

Circle two words in each sentence that could be replaced by the contraction.

She's
She is searching for clues.

It's
It is time to go home.

won't
Blenda will not give up.

can't
I can not wait to play the game.

wasn't
The customer was not happy.

hasn't
The question has not been answered.

INVESTIGATING SECOND GRADE 45

Page 45

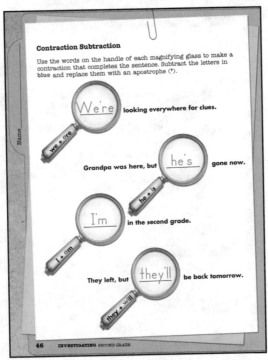

Page 46

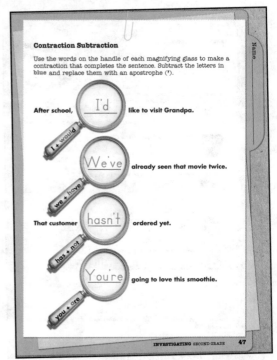

Page 47

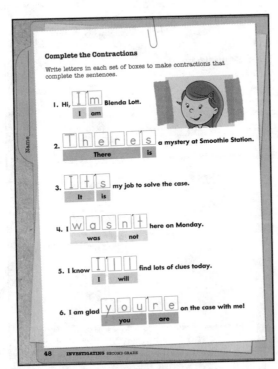

Page 48

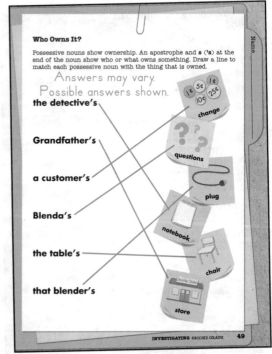

Page 49

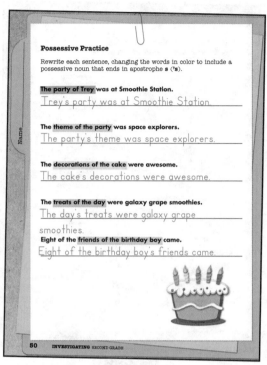

Page 50

Possessive Practice

Rewrite each sentence, changing the words in color to include a possessive noun that ends in apostrophe **s** (**'s**).

The party of Trey was at Smoothie Station.
Trey's party was at Smoothie Station.

The theme of the party was space explorers.
The party's theme was space explorers.

The decorations of the cake were awesome.
The cake's decorations were awesome.

The treats of the day were galaxy grape smoothies.
The day's treats were galaxy grape smoothies.

Eight of the friends of the birthday boy came.
Eight of the birthday boy's friends came.

50 INVESTIGATING SECOND GRADE

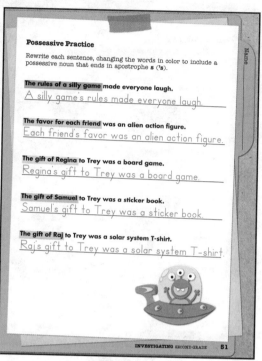

Page 51

Possessive Practice

Rewrite each sentence, changing the words in color to include a possessive noun that ends in apostrophe **s** (**'s**).

The rules of a silly game made everyone laugh.
A silly game's rules made everyone laugh.

The favor for each friend was an alien action figure.
Each friend's favor was an alien action figure.

The gift of Regina to Trey was a board game.
Regina's gift to Trey was a board game.

The gift of Samuel to Trey was a sticker book.
Samuel's gift to Trey was a sticker book.

The gift of Raj to Trey was a solar system T-shirt.
Raj's gift to Trey was a solar system T-shirt.

INVESTIGATING SECOND GRADE 51

Page 52

Where Does the Apostrophe Go?

Circle the correct phrase to describe ownership.

the store's sign
~~the stores sign's~~

~~the astronauts suits'~~
the astronaut's suit

~~the planets ring's~~
the planet's rings

~~the cakes frostings~~
the cake's frosting

the alien's ship
~~the aliens ship's~~

~~the gifts bow's~~
the gift's bow

52 INVESTIGATING SECOND GRADE

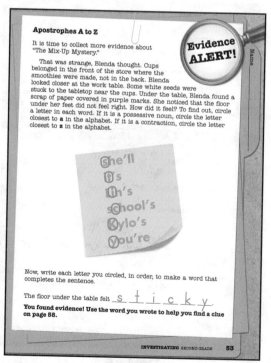

Page 53

Apostrophes A to Z

Evidence ALERT!

It is time to collect more evidence about "The Mix-Up Mystery."

That was strange, Blenda thought. Cups belonged in the front of the store where the smoothies were made, not in the back. Blenda looked closer at the work table. Some white seeds were stuck to the tabletop near the cups. Under the table, Blenda found a scrap of paper covered in purple marks. She noticed that the floor under her feet did not feel right. How did it feel? To find out, circle a letter in each word. If it is a possessive noun, circle the letter closest to **a** in the alphabet. If it is a contraction, circle the letter closest to **z** in the alphabet.

(S)he'll
I(t)'s
(I)h's
s(c)hool's
(K)ylo's
(Y)ou're

Now, write each letter you circled, in order, to make a word that completes the sentence.

The floor under the table felt s t i c k y.

You found evidence! Use the word you wrote to help you find a clue on page 58.

INVESTIGATING SECOND GRADE 53

ANSWER KEY

Page 54

In the Bag

Write the words on the bags in ABC order.

grapes
bread
soup
apples

<u>apples</u>
<u>bread</u>
<u>grapes</u>
<u>soup</u>

napkins
rolls
ice cream
pizza

<u>ice cream</u>
<u>napkins</u>
<u>pizza</u>
<u>rolls</u>

carrots
bananas
treats
potatoes

<u>bananas</u>
<u>carrots</u>
<u>potatoes</u>
<u>treats</u>

rice
soda
cups
beans

<u>beans</u>
<u>cups</u>
<u>rice</u>
<u>soda</u>

54 INVESTIGATING SECOND GRADE

Page 55

In Order

Write the words on the lines in ABC order. If two words start with the same letter, look at the second letter in each word.

tree
branch
leaf

<u>branch</u>
<u>leaf</u>
<u>tree</u>

rain
umbrella
cloud

<u>cloud</u>
<u>rain</u>
<u>umbrella</u>

dish
dog
bone

<u>bone</u>
<u>dish</u>
<u>dog</u>

mail
stamp
slot

<u>mail</u>
<u>slot</u>
<u>stamp</u>

INVESTIGATING SECOND GRADE 55

Page 56

Look It Up!

Use the dictionary page to answer the questions.

smelly (*adj.*) Having a bad odor. smell•y
smile (*noun*) A happy or pleased expression in which a person's lips are curved up. (*verb*) To form a smile by curving the lips up. smile
smock (*noun*) A long, loose piece of fabric worn over clothes to protect them. smock
smog (*noun*) A mixture of fog and smoke. smog

smoky (*adj.*) Full of smoke or giving off smoke. smok•y
smolder (*verb*) To burn slowly without flames. smol•der
smooth (*adj.*) 1. Not rough or uneven. 2. Moving without sudden stops and starts. (*verb*) To make smooth. smooth
smoothie (*noun*) A drink made by blending fruit, ice, and other ingredients. smooth•ie

What is worn to protect clothes? <u>smock</u>

What word could you use to describe a car ride with no sudden stops or starts? <u>smooth</u>

What word names an expression you might see on someone's face? <u>smile</u>

How many syllables does smoothie have? <u>2</u>

What word spells the long i sound i-consonant-e? <u>smile</u>

56 INVESTIGATING SECOND GRADE

Page 57

Look It Up!

Use the dictionary page to answer the questions.

muss (*verb*) To make messy or untidy. muss
mustache (*noun*) Hair growing on the upper lip. mus•tache
mustard (*noun*) A spicy sauce made from the seeds of the mustard plant. mus•tard
musty (*adj.*) Having a damp and rotten smell. must•y
mute (*adj.*) Silent or unspoken. (*noun*) A device used to soften the sound of a musical

instrument. (*verb*) To muffle or soften sound. mute
mutt (*noun*) A mixed-breed dog. mutt
mystery (*noun*) 1. Something that is not understood or is kept a secret. 2. A story about uncovering a secret. mys•ter•y
myth (*noun*) A very old story. myth

What is a sauce to put on food? <u>mustard</u>

What word could you use to describe a dark, wet place? <u>musty</u>

What word might a musician use? <u>mute</u>

How many syllables does mystery have? <u>3</u>

What two-syllable word ends with the long e sound? <u>musty</u>

INVESTIGATING SECOND GRADE 57

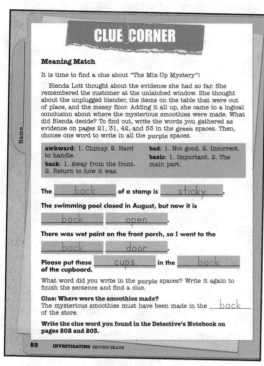

Page 58

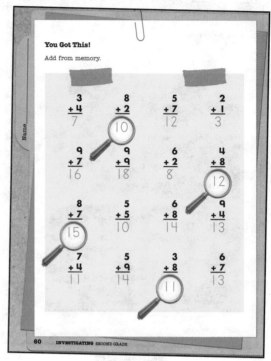

Page 60

Page 61

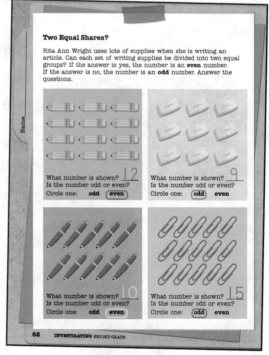

Page 62

Page 63

Two Equal Shares?

Can each set of writing supplies be divided into two equal groups? Answer the questions.

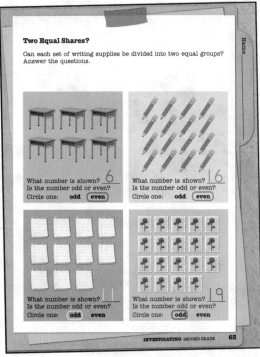

What number is shown? 6
Is the number odd or even?
Circle one: odd   (even)

What number is shown? 16
Is the number odd or even?
Circle one: odd   (even)

What number is shown? 11
Is the number odd or even?
Circle one: (odd)   even

What number is shown? 19
Is the number odd or even?
Circle one: (odd)   even

INVESTIGATING SECOND GRADE   63

Page 63

Page 64

One Left Over?

Circle pairs of objects in each set. Is one object left over? Complete the equation to show the number. Write the same addends (doubles) in the blanks. Then, answer the question. The first one is done for you.

2 + 2 + 1 = 5
Is the number odd or even?
Circle one: (odd)   even

6 + 6 = 12
Is the number odd or even?
Circle one: odd   (even)

9 + 9 = 18
Is the number odd or even?
Circle one: odd   (even)

3 + 3 + 1 = 7
Is the number odd or even?
Circle one: (odd)   even

64   INVESTIGATING SECOND GRADE

Page 64

Page 65

One Left Over?

Circle pairs of objects in each set. Is one object left over? Complete the equation to show the number. Write the same addends (doubles) in the blanks. Then, answer the question.

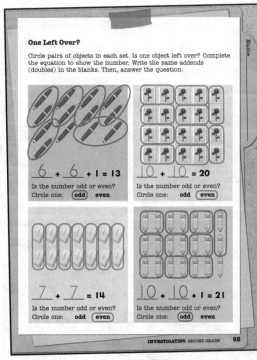

6 + 6 + 1 = 13
Is the number odd or even?
Circle one: (odd)   even

10 + 10 = 20
Is the number odd or even?
Circle one: odd   (even)

7 + 7 = 14
Is the number odd or even?
Circle one: odd   (even)

10 + 10 + 1 = 21
Is the number odd or even?
Circle one: (odd)   even

INVESTIGATING SECOND GRADE   65

Page 65

Page 66

Color Chart

Color the even numbers red. Color the odd numbers blue.

1	2	3	4	5
6	7	8	9	10
11	12	13	14	15
16	17	18	19	20
21	22	23	24	25

66   INVESTIGATING SECOND GRADE

Page 66

ANSWER KEY

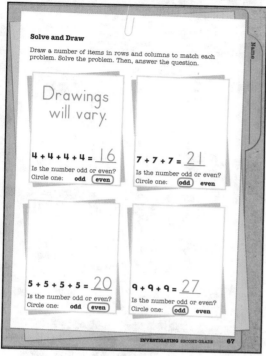

Solve and Draw

Draw a number of items in rows and columns to match each problem. Solve the problem. Then, answer the question.

Drawings will vary.

$4 + 4 + 4 + 4 = \underline{16}$

Is the number odd or even?
Circle one: odd   (even)

$7 + 7 + 7 = \underline{21}$

Is the number odd or even?
Circle one: (odd)   even

$5 + 5 + 5 + 5 = \underline{20}$

Is the number odd or even?
Circle one: odd   (even)

$9 + 9 + 9 = \underline{27}$

Is the number odd or even?
Circle one: (odd)   even

INVESTIGATING SECOND GRADE   67

Page 67

An Even Count

It is time to collect more evidence about "The Mix-Up Mystery."

Evidence ALERT!

I know where the mystery smoothies were made, thought Blenda, but who made them? Just then, the newspaper reporter Rita Ann Wright came bustling into the store's back room. "Hello, dear," she said to Blenda as she pulled a notebook and a blue pen from her bag. "I know your grandfather isn't here, but I need to work on my article. I'll just have a look around." Ms. Wright began to pick things up. "What is this?" she asked as she held up a whisk. "I've never seen one before." How many things did Ms. Wright pick up? To find out, circle the even numbers.

Write the sum of the numbers you circled to complete the sentence.

Rita Ann Wright picked up __24__ things in the back room of Smoothie Station.

You found evidence! Use the number you wrote to help you find a clue on page 106.

68   INVESTIGATING SECOND GRADE

Page 68

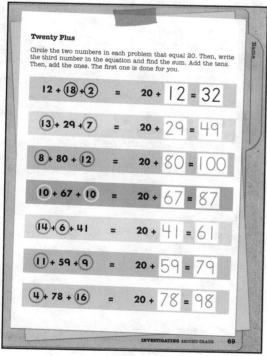

Twenty Plus

Circle the two numbers in each problem that equal 20. Then, write the third number in the equation and find the sum. Add the tens. Then, add the ones. The first one is done for you.

$12 + (18) + (2) = 20 + \boxed{12} = \boxed{32}$

$(13) + 29 + (7) = 20 + \boxed{29} = \boxed{49}$

$(8) + 80 + (12) = 20 + \boxed{80} = \boxed{100}$

$(10) + 67 + (10) = 20 + \boxed{67} = \boxed{87}$

$(14) + (6) + 41 = 20 + \boxed{41} = \boxed{61}$

$(11) + 59 + (9) = 20 + \boxed{59} = \boxed{79}$

$(4) + 78 + (16) = 20 + \boxed{78} = \boxed{98}$

INVESTIGATING SECOND GRADE   69

Page 69

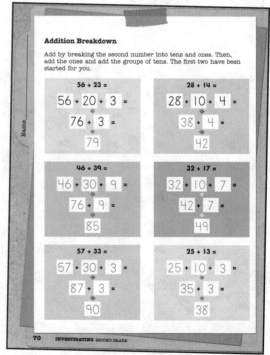

Addition Breakdown

Add by breaking the second number into tens and ones. Then, add the ones and add the groups of tens. The first two have been started for you.

$56 + 23 =$
$56 + 20 + 3 =$
$76 + 3 =$
79

$28 + 14 =$
$28 + 10 + 4 =$
$38 + 4 =$
42

$46 + 39 =$
$46 + 30 + 9 =$
$76 + 9 =$
85

$32 + 17 =$
$32 + 10 + 7 =$
$42 + 7 =$
49

$57 + 33 =$
$57 + 30 + 3 =$
$87 + 3 =$
90

$25 + 13 =$
$25 + 10 + 3 =$
$35 + 3 =$
38

70   INVESTIGATING SECOND GRADE

Page 70

Page 71

Subtraction Square

Use the hundred board to help you subtract. Put your finger on the first number. Count back the number of squares shown by the second number to find the difference.

31	57	19	77	99	88
− 10	− 13	− 8	− 12	− 6	− 10
21	44	11	65	93	78

22	67	36	88	94	51
− 11	− 14	− 9	− 12	− 5	− 12
11	53	27	76	89	39

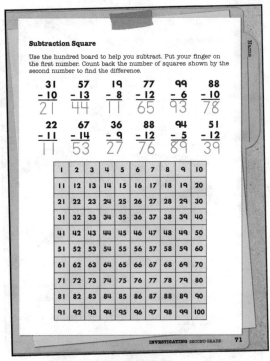

1	2	3	4	5	6	7	8	9	10
11	12	13	14	15	16	17	18	19	20
21	22	23	24	25	26	27	28	29	30
31	32	33	34	35	36	37	38	39	40
41	42	43	44	45	46	47	48	49	50
51	52	53	54	55	56	57	58	59	60
61	62	63	64	65	66	67	68	69	70
71	72	73	74	75	76	77	78	79	80
81	82	83	84	85	86	87	88	89	90
91	92	93	94	95	96	97	98	99	100

INVESTIGATING SECOND GRADE   71

Page 72

Ones, Then Tens

To solve each problem, add or subtract the ones. Then, add or subtract the tens. Regroup tens as needed.

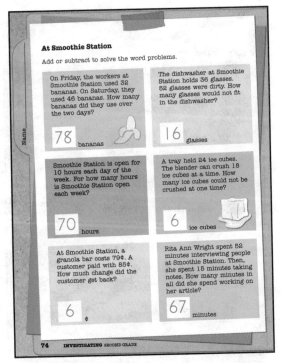

45	23	38	57
+ 37	− 5	+ 46	+ 15
82	18	84	72

80	85	55	63
− 42	− 37	+ 6	− 57
38	48	61	6

83	64	94	64
− 9	+ 27	− 67	+ 27
74	91	27	91

77	44	52	12
− 19	+ 19	− 24	+ 48
58	63	28	60

72   INVESTIGATING SECOND GRADE

Page 73

Ones, Then Tens

To solve each problem, add or subtract the ones. Then, add or subtract the tens. Regroup tens as needed.

66	33	40	17
+ 9	+ 8	− 18	+ 56
75	41	22	73

66	32	29	54
− 59	− 8	+ 28	− 49
7	24	57	5

36	76	70	93
+ 47	+ 19	− 21	− 65
83	95	49	28

18	33	83	67
+ 26	− 16	− 47	+ 17
44	17	36	84

INVESTIGATING SECOND GRADE   73

Page 74

At Smoothie Station

Add or subtract to solve the word problems.

On Friday, the workers at Smoothie Station used 32 bananas. On Saturday, they used 46 bananas. How many bananas did they use over the two days?

78 bananas

The dishwasher at Smoothie Station holds 36 glasses. 52 glasses were dirty. How many glasses would not fit in the dishwasher?

16 glasses

Smoothie Station is open for 10 hours each day of the week. For how many hours is Smoothie Station open each week?

70 hours

A tray held 24 ice cubes. The blender can crush 18 ice cubes at a time. How many ice cubes could not be crushed at one time?

6 ice cubes

At Smoothie Station, a granola bar costs 79¢. A customer paid with 85¢. How much change did the customer get back?

6 ¢

Rita Ann Wright spent 52 minutes interviewing people at Smoothie Station. Then, she spent 15 minutes taking notes. How many minutes in all did she spend working on her article?

67 minutes

74   INVESTIGATING SECOND GRADE

Page 75

At Smoothie Station

Add or subtract to solve the word problems.

Blenda Lott is 9 years old. Rita Ann Wright is 27 years old. How much older is Ms. Wright?

18 years

A truck brought 26 boxes of supplies on Monday and 37 boxes of supplies on Friday. How many boxes of supplies were delivered in all?

63 boxes

A school class with 26 students visited Smoothie Station. The workers had prepared 32 treats for them. How many treats were left over?

6 treats

Rita Ann Wright has 96 hours to finish her story about Smoothie Station. She has been working on the story for 68 hours. How many hours does she have left?

28 hours

On a Saturday, 32 customers ordered a smoothie with strawberries. 58 customers ordered a smoothie without strawberries. How many customers ordered a smoothie on that day?

90 customers

A gumball machine in the shop holds 75 gumballs. 48 gumballs are in the machine. How many gumballs have been sold since the machine was full?

27 gumballs

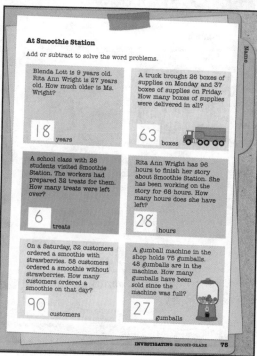

INVESTIGATING SECOND GRADE 75

Page 76

Sum Smoothie!

Evidence ALERT!

It is time to collect more evidence about "The Mix-Up Mystery."

Rita Ann Wright kept snooping around and scribbling notes. As she bent to look under a shelf, a take-out menu fell from her bag. "Thanks," said Ms. Wright when Blenda picked it up. "I will need that. I never have time to cook!"

"Have you ever made a smoothie?" asked Blenda.

"Yes! Your grandfather showed me how on Sunday. It was fun tossing all kinds of fruits into the blender. It was my own unique creation. And the taste was fascinating!"

"How many different ingredients did you put in?" asked Blenda. To find the answer, write numbers in the squares so that the sum of each row, column, and diagonal is the same.

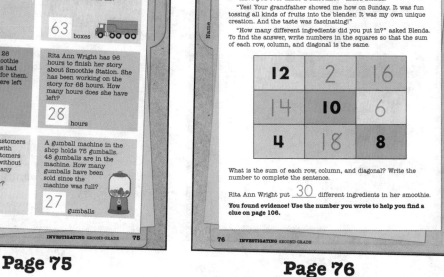

12	2	16
14	10	6
4	18	8

What is the sum of each row, column, and diagonal? Write the number to complete the sentence.

Rita Ann Wright put __30__ different ingredients in her smoothie.

You found evidence! Use the number you wrote to help you find a clue on page 106.

76 INVESTIGATING SECOND GRADE

Page 77

Ten Tens Is 100

Ten tens equal 100. Look at each group of hundreds blocks. Write the number shown. The first one is done for you. Hint: Each number you write will end with 00.

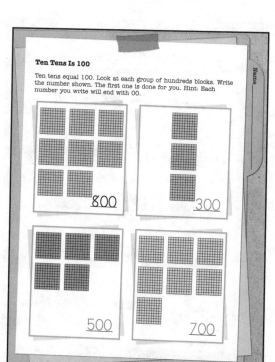

800

300

500

700

INVESTIGATING SECOND GRADE 77

Page 78

Three Places

Write the three-digit number shown by each set of blocks. The first one is done for you.

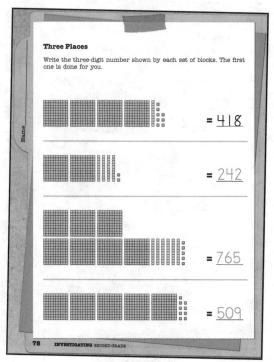

= **418**

= **242**

= **765**

= **509**

78 INVESTIGATING SECOND GRADE

Three Places

Write the three-digit number shown by each set of blocks.

= <u>643</u>

= <u>910</u>

= <u>84</u>

= <u>999</u>

INVESTIGATING SECOND GRADE   79

Page 79

Make It Big!

Write each set of three numbers in the boxes. Choose the order for the digits that will make the largest number possible.

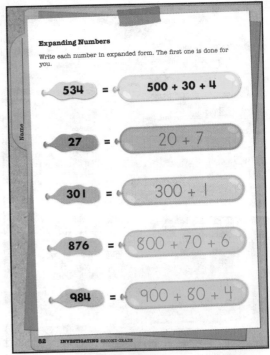

0, 6, 4

| 6 | 4 | 0 |
| Hundreds | Tens | Ones |

5, 9, 1

| 9 | 5 | 1 |
| Hundreds | Tens | Ones |

8, 2, 6

| 8 | 6 | 2 |
| Hundreds | Tens | Ones |

3, 0, 7

| 7 | 3 | 0 |
| Hundreds | Tens | Ones |

2, 0, 4

| 4 | 2 | 0 |
| Hundreds | Tens | Ones |

2, 6, 8

| 8 | 6 | 2 |
| Hundreds | Tens | Ones |

80   INVESTIGATING SECOND GRADE

Page 80

Make It Small!

Write each set of three numbers in the boxes. Choose the order for the digits that will make the smallest number possible. Hint: If you decide to write 0 in the hundreds place or the tens place, you can leave that box blank.

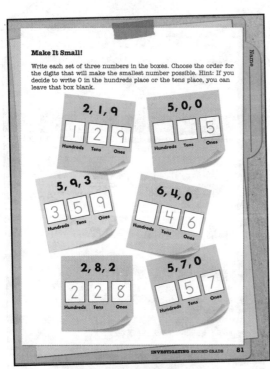

2, 1, 9

| 1 | 2 | 9 |
| Hundreds | Tens | Ones |

5, 0, 0

| | | 5 |
| Hundreds | Tens | Ones |

5, 9, 3

| 3 | 5 | 9 |
| Hundreds | Tens | Ones |

6, 4, 0

| | 4 | 6 |
| Hundreds | Tens | Ones |

2, 8, 2

| 2 | 2 | 8 |
| Hundreds | Tens | Ones |

5, 7, 0

| | 5 | 7 |
| Hundreds | Tens | Ones |

INVESTIGATING SECOND GRADE   81

Page 81

Expanding Numbers

Write each number in expanded form. The first one is done for you.

534 = 500 + 30 + 4

27 = 20 + 7

301 = 300 + 1

876 = 800 + 70 + 6

984 = 900 + 80 + 4

82   INVESTIGATING SECOND GRADE

Page 82

ANSWER KEY

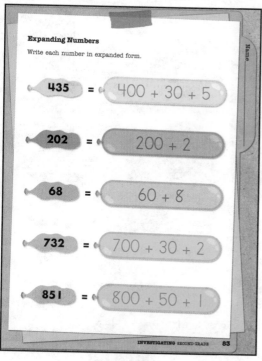

Page 83

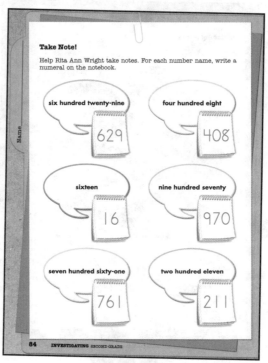

Page 84

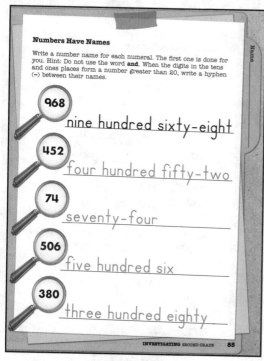

Page 85

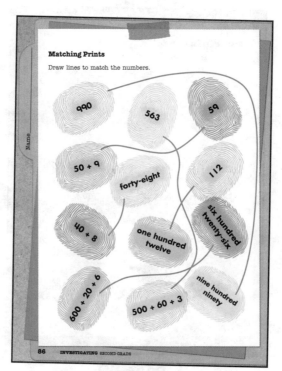

Page 86

ANSWER KEY

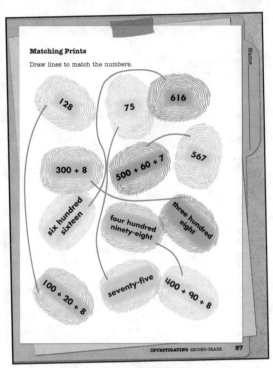

Page 87

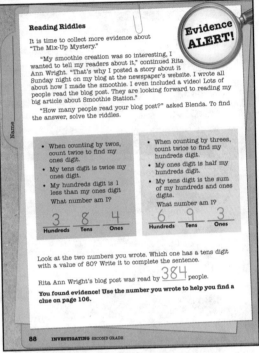

Page 88

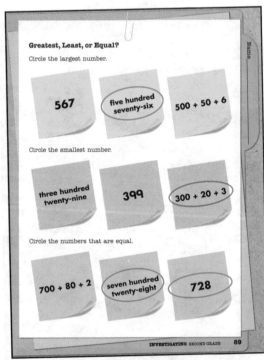

Page 89

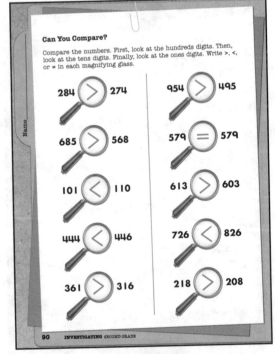

Page 90

Can You Compare?

Compare the numbers. Write >, <, or = in each magnifying glass.

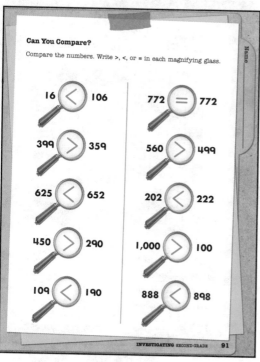

16 < 106   772 = 772

399 > 359   560 > 499

625 < 652   202 < 222

450 > 290   1,000 > 100

109 < 190   888 < 898

INVESTIGATING SECOND GRADE   91

Page 91

10 More

Yummy toppings are kept in jars at Smoothie Station. Look at the number on the first jar in each pair. On the second jar, write a number that is 10 more.

50 60   36 46

124 134   89 99

654 664   278 288

92   INVESTIGATING SECOND GRADE

Page 92

100 More

Look at the number on the first jar in each pair. On the second jar, write a number that is 100 more.

12 112   76 176

238 338   841 941

22 122   508 608

INVESTIGATING SECOND GRADE   93

Page 93

What's Next?

Write the missing numbers to complete the pattern in each row.

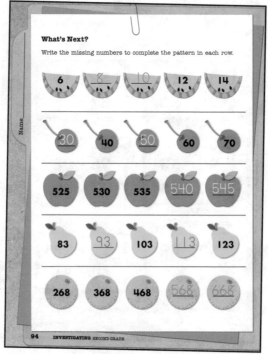

6 8 10 12 14

30 40 50 60 70

525 530 535 540 545

83 93 103 113 123

268 368 468 568 668

94   INVESTIGATING SECOND GRADE

Page 94

What's Next?

Write the missing numbers to complete the pattern in each row.

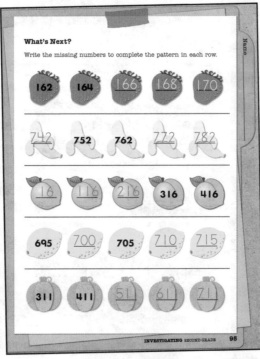

162   164   166   168   170

742   752   762   772   782

16   116   216   316   416

695   700   705   710   715

311   411   511   611   711

Page 95

One Thousand

The chart shows how to count to 1,000 by tens. Use it to answer the questions.

10	20	30	40	50	60	70	80	90	100
110	120	130	140	150	160	170	180	190	200
210	220	230	240	250	260	270	280	290	300
310	320	330	340	350	360	370	380	390	400
410	420	430	440	450	460	470	480	490	500
510	520	530	540	550	560	570	580	590	600
610	620	630	640	650	660	670	680	690	700
710	720	730	740	750	760	770	780	790	800
810	820	830	840	850	860	870	880	890	900
910	920	930	940	950	960	970	980	990	1,000

What is 200 less than 670? _____ 470

What is 300 more than 530? _____ 830

What is 30 more than 130? _____ 160

What is 80 less than 690? _____ 610

What is 500 more than 500? _____ 1,000

Page 96

Rita's Readers

Add the numbers on each computer monitor to find out how many readers visited Rita's website that day. Regroup as needed.

38   16
75   50

Readers on Day #1: 179

59   15
82   46

Readers on Day #2: 202

90   50
60   45

Readers on Day #3: 245

26   88
47   19

Readers on Day #4: 180

62   79
85   93

Readers on Day #5: 319

12   28
64   51

Readers on Day #6: 155

Page 97

Comment Count

Evidence ALERT!

It is time to collect more evidence about "The Mix-Up Mystery."

"Not only did lots of people read the blog post about the smoothie I made," Rita continued, "but lots of people left nice comments, too. They said that my smoothie creation sounded so creative and unusual. I think they all wanted to try it for themselves!"

"How many people left comments on your website?" asked Blenda Lott. To find the answer, add the numbers on each group of four mice.

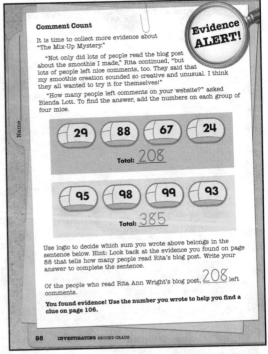

29   88   67   24

Total: 208

95   98   99   93

Total: 385

Use logic to decide which sum you wrote above belongs in the sentence below. Hint: Look back at the evidence you found on page 88 that tells how many people read Rita's blog post. Write your answer to complete the sentence.

Of the people who read Rita Ann Wright's blog post, 208 left comments.

You found evidence! Use the number you wrote to help you find a clue on page 106.

Page 98

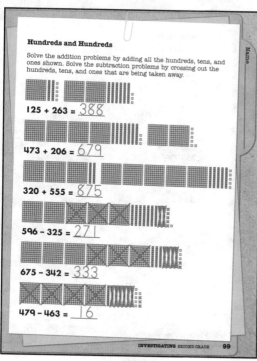

Hundreds and Hundreds

Solve the addition problems by adding all the hundreds, tens, and ones shown. Solve the subtraction problems by crossing out the hundreds, tens, and ones that are being taken away.

125 + 263 = _388_

473 + 206 = _679_

320 + 555 = _875_

596 − 325 = _271_

675 − 342 = _333_

479 − 463 = _16_

INVESTIGATING SECOND GRADE 99

Page 99

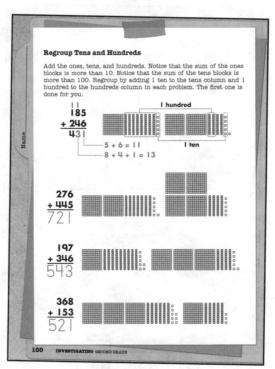

Regroup Tens and Hundreds

Add the ones, tens, and hundreds. Notice that the sum of the ones blocks is more than 10. Notice that the sum of the tens blocks is more than 100. Regroup by adding 1 ten to the tens column and 1 hundred to the hundreds column in each problem. The first one is done for you.

```
  11
  185          I hundred
+ 246
  431
        5 + 6 = 11       I ten
        8 + 4 + 1 = 13
```

```
  276
+ 445
  721
```

```
  197
+ 346
  543
```

```
  368
+ 153
  521
```

100 INVESTIGATING SECOND GRADE

Page 100

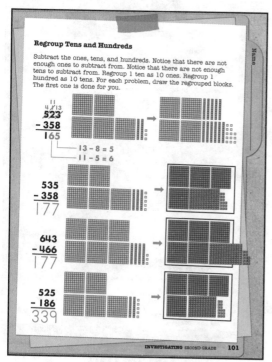

Regroup Tens and Hundreds

Subtract the ones, tens, and hundreds. Notice that there are not enough ones to subtract from. Notice that there are not enough tens to subtract from. Regroup 1 ten as 10 ones. Regroup 1 hundred as 10 tens. For each problem, draw the regrouped blocks. The first one is done for you.

```
  11  13
  4  X 13
  523
− 358
  165
        13 − 8 = 5
        11 − 5 = 6
```

```
  535
− 358
  177
```

```
  643
− 466
  177
```

```
  525
− 186
  339
```

INVESTIGATING SECOND GRADE 101

Page 101

Delivery Day

Boxes of supplies were delivered to Smoothie Station. Choose numbers from the boxes to write in the blanks. Then, solve the problems you made!

Problems will vary.

187   299   364
To: Smoothie Station   89   576
402   56   100

102 INVESTIGATING SECOND GRADE

Page 102

Page 103

Delivery Day

Boxes of supplies were delivered to Smoothie Station. Choose numbers from the boxes to write in the blanks. Then, solve the problems you made!

Problems will vary.

688 99 105 52 136 754 951 357

What's the Problem?

Add or subtract. Regroup tens and hundreds as needed.

425	711	719	186
+ 125	+ 191	− 532	− 92
550	902	187	94

432	300	213	862
− 257	+ 547	+ 519	− 541
175	847	732	321

650	159	86	137
+ 129	− 82	+ 93	+ 310
779	77	179	447

519	909	76	411
− 120	− 457	+ 192	+ 120
399	452	268	531

Page 104

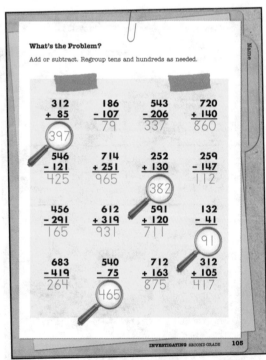

What's the Problem?

Add or subtract. Regroup tens and hundreds as needed.

312	186	543	720
+ 85	− 107	− 206	+ 140
397	79	337	860

546	714	252	259
− 121	+ 251	+ 130	− 147
425	965	382	112

456	612	591	132
− 291	+ 319	+ 120	− 41
165	931	711	91

683	540	712	312
− 419	− 75	+ 163	+ 105
264	465	875	417

Page 105

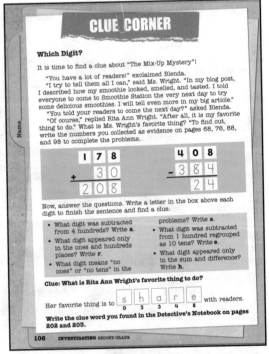

CLUE CORNER

Which Digit?

It is time to find a clue about "The Mix-Up Mystery"!

"You have a lot of readers!" exclaimed Blenda.

"I try to tell them all I can," said Ms. Wright. "In my blog post, I described how my smoothie looked, smelled, and tasted. I told everyone to come to Smoothie Station the very next day to try some delicious smoothies. I will tell even more in my big article."

"You told your readers to come the next day?" asked Blenda.

"Of course," replied Rita Ann Wright. "After all, it is my favorite thing to do." What is Ms. Wright's favorite thing? "To find out, write the numbers you collected as evidence on pages 68, 76, 88, and 98 to complete the problems.

1	7	8		4	0	8
+	3	0	−	3	8	4
2	0	8			2	4

Now, answer the questions. Write a letter in the box above each digit to finish the sentence and find a clue.

- What digit was subtracted from 4 hundreds? Write **a**.
- What digit appeared only in the ones and hundreds places? Write **r**.
- What digit means "no ones" or "no tens" in the problems? Write **s**.
- What digit was subtracted from 1 hundred regrouped as 10 tens? Write **e**.
- What digit appeared only in the sum and difference? Write **h**.

Clue: What is Rita Ann Wright's favorite thing to do?

Her favorite thing is to [s 0] [h 2] [a 3] [r 4] [e 8] with readers.

Write the clue word you found in the Detective's Notebook on pages 202 and 203.

Page 106

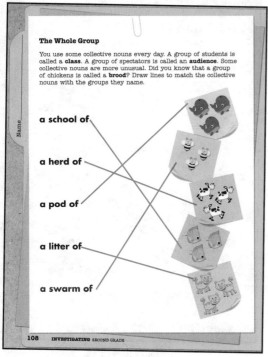

Page 108

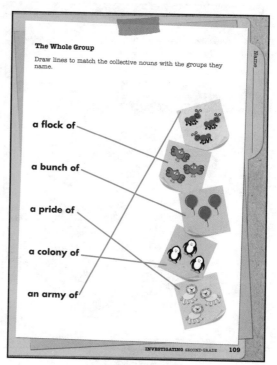

Page 109

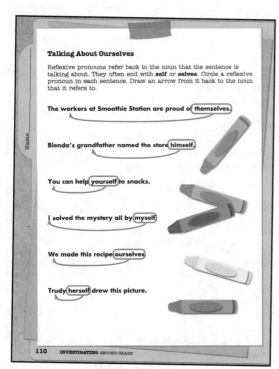

Page 110

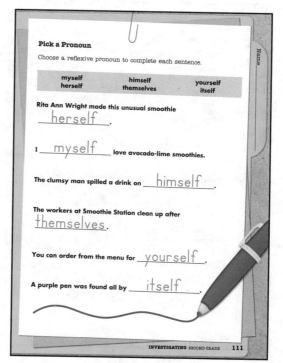

Page 111

ANSWER KEY

Page 112

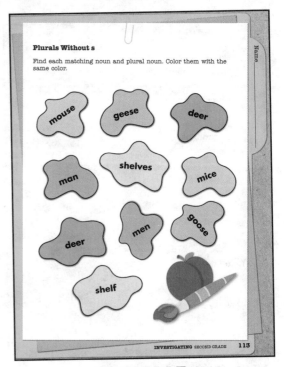

Page 113

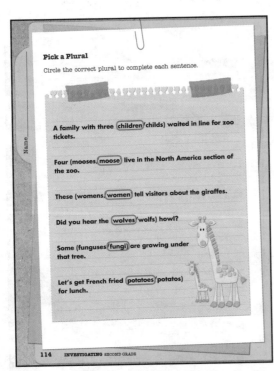

Page 114

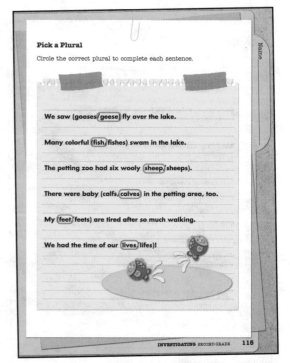

Page 115

Plurals and Projects

It is time to collect more evidence about "The Mix-Up Mystery."

Evidence ALERT!

Ms. Wright had to go, so Blenda found Trudy Culors, who was helping a customer. "I'm glad you are here!" said Blenda. "Grandpa said you were here yesterday, too."

"I was! I had time to work on my new art project," said Trudy.

"What is it?" asked Blenda.

"Making smoothies! Your grandfather said I could use leftover ingredients to mix drinks with crazy new colors. I noticed how mixing fruits and vegetables is kind of like mixing..." What does Trudy think mixing fruits and vegetables is like? To find out, circle seven plurals in the puzzle. Write them on the lines. Hint: They may be regular or irregular plurals.

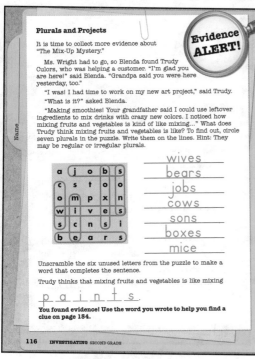

wives
bears
jobs
cows
sons
boxes
mice

Unscramble the six unused letters from the puzzle to make a word that completes the sentence.

Trudy thinks that mixing fruits and vegetables is like mixing

p a i n t s .

You found evidence! Use the word you wrote to help you find a clue on page 154.

116   INVESTIGATING SECOND GRADE

Page 116

Irregular Verbs

Some verbs do not follow the patterns you know. Their past-tense forms do not end with **ed**. Use the verbs in the magnifying glasses to complete the sentences.

1. When Trudy has a thoughtful look on her face, she ____is____ probably thinking about her next art project.

2. Trudy and Blenda ____were____ talking about what happened on Monday.

3. Blenda ____was____ not here when the mystery smoothies were made.

4. The customers at Smoothie Station ____were____ unhappy that they could not order the new drink.

*is
was
were*

1. Blenda is ____going____ to solve the mystery.

2. Where did Rita Ann Wright ____go____?

3. Many customers ____went____ to Smoothie Station last weekend.

4. Trudy is ____going____ to mix fruits and vegetables.

*go
going
went*

INVESTIGATING SECOND GRADE   117

Page 117

Irregular Verbs

Some verbs do not follow the patterns you know. Their past-tense forms do not end with **ed**. Use the verbs in the magnifying glasses to complete the sentences.

1. Smoothies ____have____ many ingredients.

2. Blenda ____has____ been visiting her grandfather at work.

3. Trudy ____has____ lots of art supplies.

4. Yesterday, Blenda ____had____ a chocolate-coconut-banana smoothie.

*have
has
had*

1. Every day, Grandpa ____sees____ many customers at his store.

2. Did anyone ____see____ who made the mystery smoothies?

3. Last week, Blenda ____saw____ Trudy Culors after school every day.

4. How many people ____saw____ Rita Ann Wright's blog post?

*see
sees
saw*

118   INVESTIGATING SECOND GRADE

Page 118

Irregular Verbs

Some verbs do not follow the patterns you know. Their past-tense forms do not end with **ed**. Use the verbs in the magnifying glasses to complete the sentences.

1. Rita Ann Wright does not have time to cook, so she ____eats____ at restaurants often.

2. Smoothie Station customers ____ate____ 50 granola bars last week.

3. Is it time to ____eat____?

4. We ____ate____ the last banana yesterday.

*eat
eats
ate*

1. Who ____left____ a purple pen on the table yesterday?

2. Rita Ann Wright had to ____leave____.

3. Blenda comes to Smoothie Station after she ____leaves____ school.

4. Three customers just ____left____.

*leave
leaves
left*

INVESTIGATING SECOND GRADE   119

Page 119

Page 120

Irregular Verbs

Some verbs do not follow the patterns you know. Their past-tense forms do not end with **ed**. Use the verbs in the magnifying glasses to complete the sentences.

1. That customer always __buys__ a peach-mango smoothie.
2. Earlier today, a boy __bought__ two gumballs.
3. A customer asked, "Can I __buy__ the same delicious smoothie I got yesterday?"
4. Last week, Trudy __bought__ new art supplies.

> buy
> buys
> bought

1. What __does__ Rita Ann Wright like to do?
2. __Do__ you think the mystery will be solved?
3. Trudy __did__ not work last Sunday.
4. Blenda's grandfather __does__ not come to the store on Mondays.

> do
> does
> did

120 **INVESTIGATING** SECOND GRADE

Page 121

Irregular Verbs

Some verbs do not follow the patterns you know. Their past-tense forms do not end with **ed**. Use the verbs in the magnifying glasses to complete the sentences.

1. Many people __come__ to Smoothie Station to get a healthy snack.
2. What time was it when Trudy __came__ to work?
3. Here __comes__ another customer.
4. Earlier, Blenda __came__ into the back room and found evidence.

> come
> comes
> came

1. Can you __find__ some fresh strawberries?
2. This afternoon, Blenda __found__ an unlatched window.
3. Blenda's grandfather often __finds__ ingredients at the farmer's market.
4. Has the answer to the puzzle been __found__ ?

> find
> finds
> found

INVESTIGATING SECOND GRADE 121

Page 122

It Describes a Noun

Adjectives describe nouns. Draw a line from each adjective to a noun that it could describe.

Answers may vary. Possible answers shown.

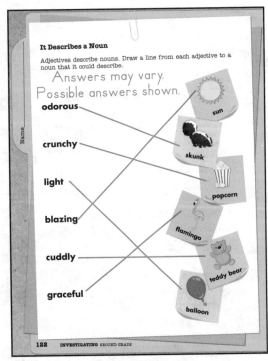

odorous · · sun
crunchy · · skunk
light · · popcorn
blazing · · flamingo
cuddly · · teddy bear
graceful · · balloon

122 **INVESTIGATING** SECOND GRADE

Page 123

It Describes a Verb

Adverbs describe verbs. They can tell how something happens. Many adverbs end with **ly**. Draw a line from each verb to an adverb that could describe it.

Answers may vary. Possible answers shown.

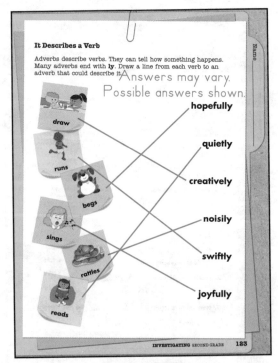

draw · · hopefully
runs · · quietly
begs · · creatively
sings · · noisily
rattles · · swiftly
reads · · joyfully

INVESTIGATING SECOND GRADE 123

ANSWER KEY

Page 124

Adjective or Adverb?

Decide whether the underlined words are nouns or verbs. Then, choose adjectives or adverbs to describe them.

Adjectives	**Adverbs**
colorful	carefully
tiny	outside
excellent	often

1. Trudy Culors is an **excellent** <u>artist</u>.

2. She <u>draws</u> and <u>paints</u> **often**.

3. Trudy has taken art classes since she was a **tiny** <u>girl</u>.

4. All of her <u>creations</u> are bright and **colorful**.

5. Trudy <u>mixes</u> colors **carefully**.

6. <u>Going</u> **outside** always gives her new ideas for projects.

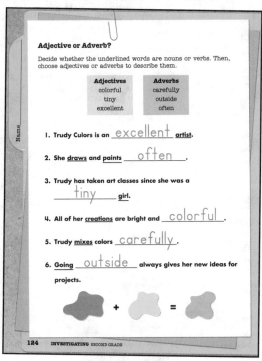

124 INVESTIGATING SECOND GRADE

Page 125

Adjective or Adverb?

Decide whether the underlined words are nouns or verbs. Then, choose adjectives or adverbs to describe them.

Adjectives	**Adverbs**
unusual	expertly
favorite	always
delicious	inside

1. Trudy likes <u>to work</u> **inside** at Smoothie Station.

2. She thinks <u>smoothies</u> are **delicious** and fun to make.

3. She likes to use **unusual** <u>ingredients</u>.

4. Trudy **expertly** <u>mixes</u> up kiwis and carrots.

5. Some of her **favorite** <u>colors</u> are yellow, red, and orange.

6. Trudy **always** <u>smiles</u> at customers.

INVESTIGATING SECOND GRADE 125

Page 126

New and Improved

Rewrite the sentences so that they tell more information. Choose adjectives and adverbs from the boxes to include in your new sentences.

Adjectives	**Adverbs**
fresh	quickly
sharp	tightly
creamy	slowly
tasty	carefully
whole	completely

1. Use limes and bananas to make this drink.
   Answers will vary.

2. Chop the ice with a blade.

3. Squeeze the lime to collect its juice.

4. Pour in the juice.

5. Stir in the bananas.

6. Clean up the kitchen when you are done.

126 INVESTIGATING SECOND GRADE

Page 127

Which Color?

Evidence ALERT!

It is time to collect more evidence about "The Mix-Up Mystery."

As Trudy talked, Blenda observed the area where the older girl had been working. It was kind of messy. Puddles of juice and ice chips stood on the counter. Trudy's sketchbook lay open to a page covered in purple doodles. "Your project sounds really interesting," said Blenda. "What new colors did you make?"

"First," said Trudy, "I tried mixing grapes and lemons." What did Trudy call the color she made? To find out, complete the adjectives on purple crayons. Complete the adverbs on yellow crayons.

easy	under	proudly	loud	rare	yearly

yearly   **u**nde**r**

rare   **p**rou**d**l**y**

lou**d**   **e**as**y**

Now, write the first letter of each word you wrote, in order from left to right, to form a made-up word that completes the sentence.

Trudy called her new color **y u r p l e**.

You found evidence! Use the word you wrote to help you find a clue on page 154.

INVESTIGATING SECOND GRADE 127

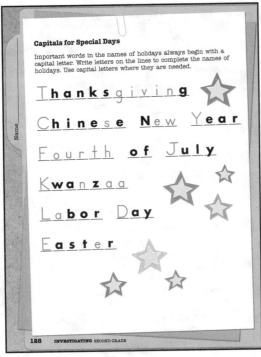

Page 128

Page 129

Page 130

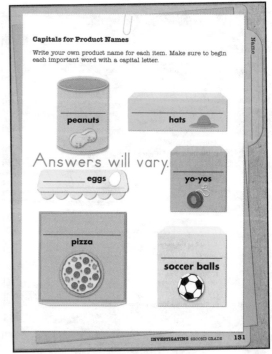

Page 131

ANSWER KEY

Page 132

Capitals for Place Names

Important words in the names of specific places begin with a capital letter. Write each place name under the category where it belongs.

Yellowstone National Park	Liberty Bell
Kansas City, Missouri	Golden Gate Bridge
Willis Tower	New York, New York
Tampa, Florida	Zion National Park
Acadia National Park	

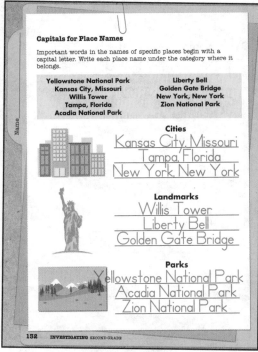

Cities
Kansas City, Missouri
Tampa, Florida
New York, New York

Landmarks
Willis Tower
Liberty Bell
Golden Gate Bridge

Parks
Yellowstone National Park
Acadia National Park
Zion National Park

132 INVESTIGATING SECOND GRADE

Page 133

Capitals for Place Names

For each category, write the names of places you know. Begin each important word with a capital letter.

Cities
_____

Landmarks
Answers will vary.

Parks
_____

INVESTIGATING SECOND GRADE 133

Page 134

Take Note!

Proofread each note. Cross out each proofreading mark in the white box as you write it in the note.

≡ Capitalize this letter.	⋀ Add a comma.	⊙ Add a period.

dear Mr Lott

Thank you for talking to our class when we came to visit Smoothie station. We enjoyed learning all about your store. We especially liked the vanilla-berry smoothies you made for us. Come and visit us at school anytime!

Sincerely,
northside Elementary School Room 212

dear Blenda

I am glad you are helping solve the mystery at smoothie Station. i know you will find the answers I need. I appreciate all your help around the shop. Let's have a yummy smoothie together soon!

Love,
Grandpa

134 INVESTIGATING SECOND GRADE

Page 135

Take Note!

Proofread each note. Cross out each proofreading mark in the white box as you write it in the note.

dear Rita ann Wright

I liked talking to you about your job. I like to tell stories with words and videos just like you do. Could I visit you at the newspaper office? Please let me know. I can't wait to read your article soon.

sincerely,
Blenda Lott

dear Mr. Tyler

I have some ideas for art projects at our school. One is to paint the fence outside in bright colors. Another is to display bright pictures of fruits and vegetables in the cafeteria. I would like to help with these projects. Thank you for being a great art teacher!

your Student,
Trudy culors

INVESTIGATING SECOND GRADE 135

Dear Mr. Lott

Write a letter to the owner of Smoothie Station, Mr. Lott. Tell him about an idea you have for a new kind of smoothie. Explain what ingredients it will have and how it will taste. Use capital letters, commas, and punctuation correctly. Proofread your letter carefully.

Letters will vary.

136 INVESTIGATING SECOND GRADE

Page 136

Commas and Colors

Evidence ALERT!

It is time to collect more evidence about "The Mix-Up Mystery."

Trudy kept talking excitedly about her project. "Next," she explained to Blenda, "I tried another wild mix-up. I used cucumbers, kiwi fruits, honeydew melons, and blueberries. It was the most amazing color I have ever seen!" What did Trudy call the new color she made? To find out, read the names of places in the world whose names include colors. Insert four commas where they are needed. Circle five letters that should be capitals.

(b)lue Mound, Texas

Yellow Pine, (l)ouisiana

(e)merald, Australia

White Cliffs of Dover, (e)ngland

Orange, California

Red Bank, (n)ew Jersey

Now, write the letters you circled, in order, to find a made-up word that completes the sentence.

Trudy called the new color she made b l e e n .

You found evidence! Use the word you wrote to help you find a clue on page 154.

INVESTIGATING SECOND GRADE 137

Page 137

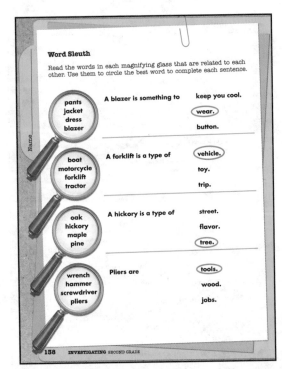

Word Sleuth

Read the words in each magnifying glass that are related to each other. Use them to circle the best word to complete each sentence.

pants jacket dress blazer	A blazer is something to	keep you cool. (wear.) button.
boat motorcycle forklift tractor	A forklift is a type of	(vehicle.) toy. trip.
oak hickory maple pine	A hickory is a type of	street. flavor. (tree.)
wrench hammer screwdriver pliers	Pliers are	(tools.) wood. jobs.

138 INVESTIGATING SECOND GRADE

Page 138

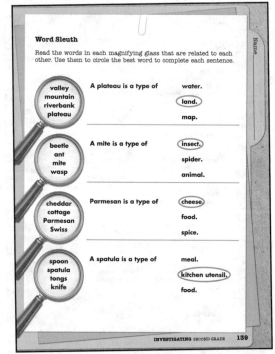

Word Sleuth

Read the words in each magnifying glass that are related to each other. Use them to circle the best word to complete each sentence.

valley mountain riverbank plateau	A plateau is a type of	water. (land.) map.
beetle ant mite wasp	A mite is a type of	(insect.) spider. animal.
cheddar cottage Parmesan Swiss	Parmesan is a type of	(cheese.) food. spice.
spoon spatula tongs knife	A spatula is a type of	meal. (kitchen utensil.) food.

INVESTIGATING SECOND GRADE 139

Page 139

Page 140

Where Does It Fit?

Write each word under the category it fits best.

magenta	cranberry	pineapple	fig
heat	blizzard	chop	whisk
raspberry	beige	hurricane	rain
thunderclap	combine	charcoal	violet

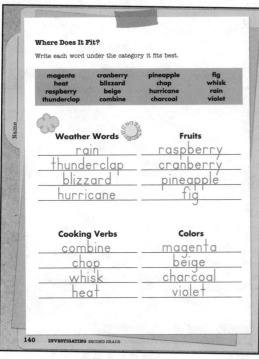

Weather Words
rain
thunderclap
blizzard
hurricane

Fruits
raspberry
cranberry
pineapple
fig

Cooking Verbs
combine
chop
whisk
heat

Colors
magenta
beige
charcoal
violet

140 INVESTIGATING SECOND GRADE

Page 141

Where Does It Fit?

Write each word under the category it fits best.

gazelle	bank	price	savings
dictionary	elephant	watercolor	sketch
payment	easel	rhinoceros	thesaurus
paintbrush	atlas	encyclopedia	bonobo

Art Words
paintbrush
easel
watercolor
sketch

African Animals
gazelle
elephant
rhinoceros
bonobo

Information Sources
dictionary
atlas
encyclopedia
thesaurus

Money Words
payment
bank
price
savings

INVESTIGATING SECOND GRADE 141

Page 142

Context Clues

Look for clues in each sentence to help you circle the meaning of the colored word.

After paying for the smoothie, the customer asked for her receipt.

money that is owed
(paper that tells how much was paid)
cash register

The store had too many bananas, and there was also a surplus of yogurt.

too little
the right amount
(too much)

Since I don't like this one, can I exchange it for another kind?

(trade)
pay for
throw away

At the price of only one dollar, that snack is a real bargain!

something that is worthless
(a good deal)
something bought with a coupon

Please deposit the mop in the closet when you are done mopping.

take out
use
(put in)

142 INVESTIGATING SECOND GRADE

Page 143

Context Clues

Look for clues in each sentence to help you circle the meaning of the colored word.

I don't have enough money to buy it, so I asked Mom for a loan.

money earned
(money borrowed)
visit to a bank

The generous man bought smoothies for all 10 children in line.

(unselfish)
old
selfish

I chewed some gum, gave some to my sister, and put the balance in my room.

package
new
(leftover amount)

The medium smoothie costs one quarter less than the large one.

a half
(a fourth)
a lot

Can I have a discount on the price of this stale cookie?

(amount subtracted)
ten more
amount added

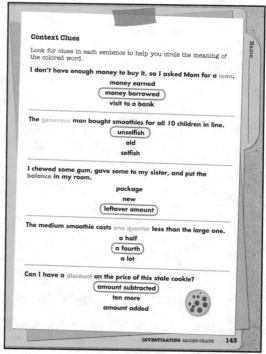

INVESTIGATING SECOND GRADE 143

Page 144

Shades of Meaning

Look at the words on each paint chip. Their meanings are similar, but not quite the same. Choose another word to write on each paint chip.

munch	run	pour	stare

peek
look
stare

trot
run
sprint

drizzle
rain
pour

nibble
munch
gobble

Page 145

Shades of Meaning

Choose another word to write on each paint chip.

terrified	thrilled	stunning	tiptoed

pretty
lovely
stunning

tiptoed
marched
strutted

scared
spooked
terrified

joyful
thrilled
delighted

Page 146

Shades of Meaning

Choose another word to write on each paint chip.

strong	super	tiny	mystery

puzzle
problem
mystery

little
tiny
miniature

strong
sturdy
everlasting

good
super
amazing

Page 147

Mystery Meanings

Evidence ALERT!

It is time to collect more evidence about "The Mix-Up Mystery."

"You are talented at mixing new colors, and at making up funny names for them," Blenda told Trudy Culors.

"Thanks!" said Trudy. "I made the cucumber-kiwi-honeydew-blueberry smoothie on Monday morning. After I admired its awesome color, I made another discovery about it. Then, I had to tell everyone I know." How did Trudy let everyone know about the smoothie she made? To find out, write a word in the puzzle to match each meaning. Write the first letter of each word in the box with the matching number. Move around the square in a spiral.

1. someone who steals
2. just right
3. feeling alone

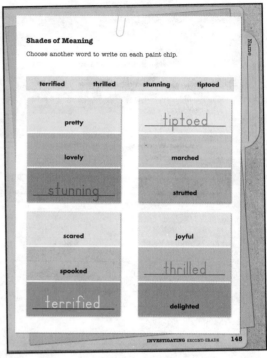

e	**f**	²e	x
i	**e**	l	**a**
h	n	**y**	**c**
¹**t**	o	³l	t

Begin at the bottom left corner and move clockwise. Write the letter you wrote in each corner of the puzzle, in order, to make a word that completes the sentence.

Trudy sent a __t e x t__ about the smoothie to everyone she knows.

You found evidence! Use the word you wrote to help you find a clue on page 154.

Page 148

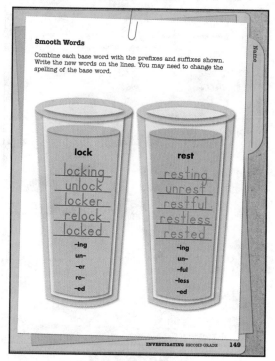

Page 149

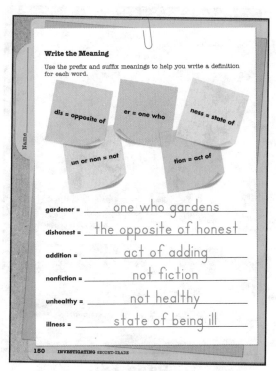

Page 150

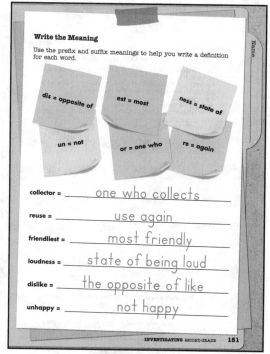

Page 151

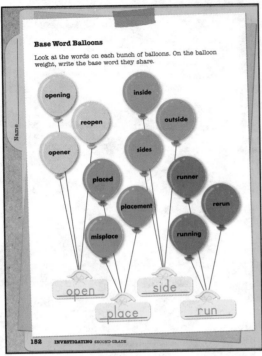

Page 152

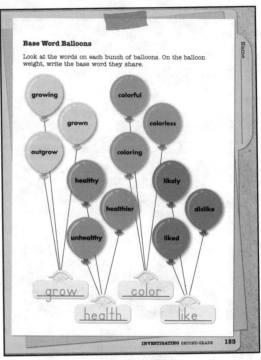

Page 153

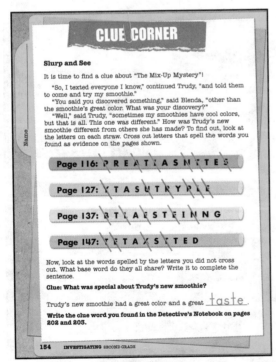

Page 154

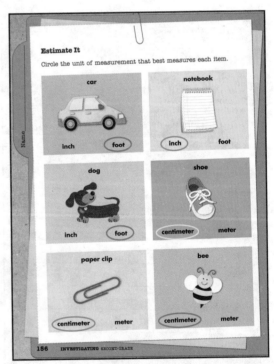

Page 156

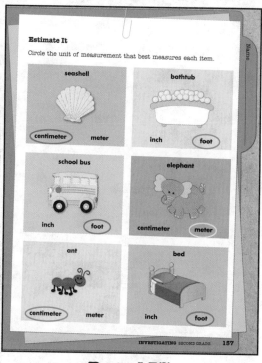

Page 157

Page 158

Page 159

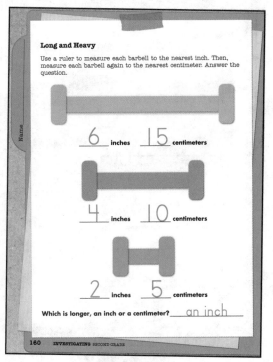

Page 160

ANSWER KEY

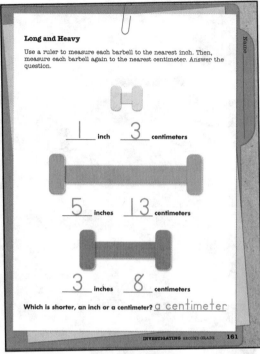

Long and Heavy

Use a ruler to measure each barbell to the nearest inch. Then, measure each barbell again to the nearest centimeter. Answer the question.

__1__ inch __3__ centimeters

__5__ inches __13__ centimeters

__3__ inches __8__ centimeters

Which is shorter, an inch or a centimeter? _a centimeter_

Page 161

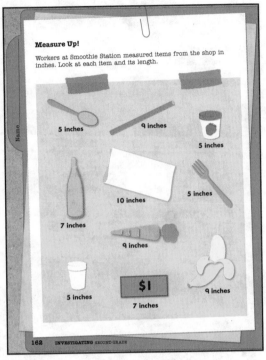

Measure Up!

Workers at Smoothie Station measured items from the shop in inches. Look at each item and its length.

5 inches 9 inches 5 inches

10 inches 5 inches

7 inches

9 inches

5 inches $1 9 inches

7 inches

Page 162

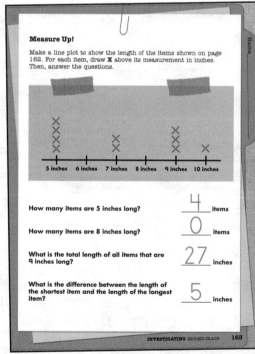

Measure Up!

Make a line plot to show the length of the items shown on page 162. For each item, draw **X** above its measurement in inches. Then, answer the questions.

```
   X
   X        X
   X   X    X
   X   X  X X   X
5   6   7  8  9  10
inches inches inches inches inches inches
```

How many items are 5 inches long? __4__ items

How many items are 8 inches long? __0__ items

What is the total length of all items that are 9 inches long? __27__ inches

What is the difference between the length of the shortest item and the length of the longest item? __5__ inches

Page 163

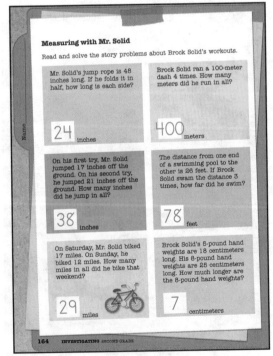

Measuring with Mr. Solid

Read and solve the story problems about Brock Solid's workouts.

Mr. Solid's jump rope is 48 inches long. If he folds it in half, how long is each side?

__24__ inches

Brock Solid ran a 100-meter dash 4 times. How many meters did he run in all?

__400__ meters

On his first try, Mr. Solid jumped 17 inches off the ground. On his second try, he jumped 21 inches off the ground. How many inches did he jump in all?

__38__ inches

The distance from one end of a swimming pool to the other is 26 feet. If Brock Solid swam the distance 3 times, how far did he swim?

__78__ feet

On Saturday, Mr. Solid biked 17 miles. On Sunday, he biked 12 miles. How many miles in all did he bike that weekend?

__29__ miles

Brock Solid's 5-pound hand weights are 18 centimeters long. His 8-pound hand weights are 25 centimeters long. How much longer are the 8-pound hand weights?

__7__ centimeters

Page 164

Inch-Up

Evidence ALERT!

It is time to collect more evidence about "The Mix-Up Mystery."

Just then, Brock Solid came into the shop, whistling. He was so tall and his shoulders were so wide that he nearly filled up the doorway. "Howdy!" he said cheerfully.

"Mr. Solid!" exclaimed Blenda. "I was hoping you'd be here today."

"I try to come every afternoon right after my workout," he explained. "You will never guess how many chin-ups I did today!" How many chin-ups did Brock Solid do? To find out, use a ruler to measure each bar to the nearest inch.

<u>4</u> inches   <u>3</u> inches   <u>2</u> inches   <u>3</u> inches

Add all the inches you measured above. Write the sum to complete the sentence.

Brock Solid did <u>12</u> chin-ups.

You found evidence! Use the number you wrote to help you find a clue on page 201.

INVESTIGATING SECOND GRADE **165**

Page 165

Two Ways to Tell Time

Draw a line to match each clock face to a digital time.

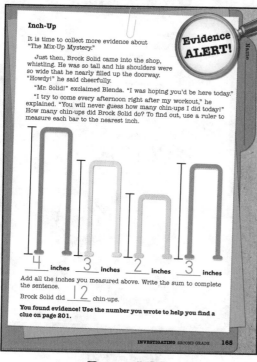

5:55

10:25

2:35

3:45

12:10

166 INVESTIGATING SECOND GRADE

Page 166

Two Ways to Tell Time

Draw a line to match each clock face to a digital time.

6:20

7:30

1:40

4:15

11:05

INVESTIGATING SECOND GRADE **167**

Page 167

What Time Is It?

Look at the time on each clock face. Write the same time on each digital clock.

6:15

9:05

4:45

8:35

168 INVESTIGATING SECOND GRADE

Page 168

Page 169

Page 170

Page 171

Page 172

ANSWER KEY

Page 173

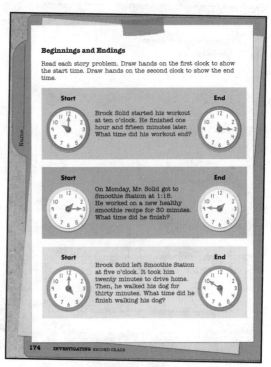

Page 174

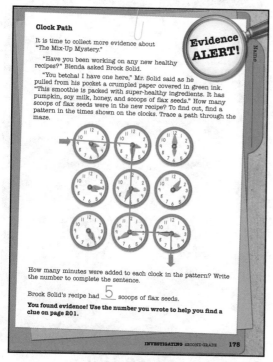

Page 175

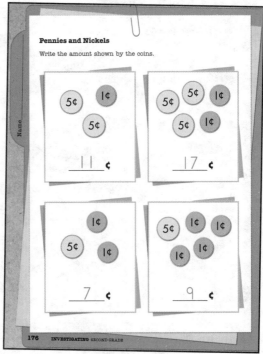

Page 176

ANSWER KEY

Page 177

Page 178

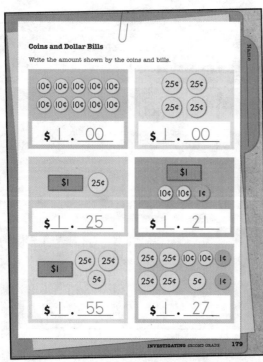

Page 179

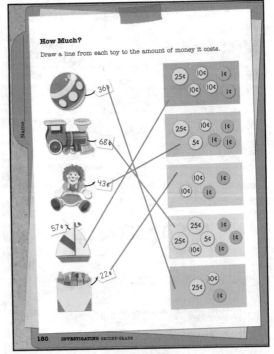

Page 180

248   **INVESTIGATING** SECOND GRADE